Seattle and Beyond:

The WTO Millennium Round

Patrick Grady

Kathleen Macmillan

Published by
Global Economics Ltd.
and
International Trade Policy
Consultants, Inc.

SEATTLE AND BEYOND: THE WTO MILLENNIUM ROUND. Copyright ©
1999 by Patrick Grady and Kathleen Macmillan.
All rights reserved / Printed in Canada

Canadian Cataloguing in Publication Data

Grady, Patrick, 1947-
Seattle and Beyond: The WTO Millennium Round
Includes biliographical references and index.

ISBN   0-9686210-0-7

1. World Trade Organization. 2. International Trade. 3. Foreign Trade Regula-
tion.
I. Macmillan, Kathleen., 1956- II. Global Economics (Firm) III. International
Trade Policy Consultants. IV. Title

HF1385.G73 1999   382'.92   C99-901479-X

Cover/Book Design & Typesetting:
Kelvin Hodges, Hodges Publications, Kemptville, Ontario
Publishing Consultant:
Elaine Kenney, Communication Matters, Ottawa, Ontario

Publisher:
Global Economics Ltd.
PO Box 927, Stn. B
Suite 307, 63 Sparks Street
Ottawa, Ontario
K1P 5S6
tel. (613) 230-7135
fax (613) 230-7576
e-mail: P_Grady@compuserve.com

Seattle and Beyond

To Jean and Graham

Table of Contents

Seattle and Beyond

Acknowledgments

We would like to thank Pierre Lortie, the President and CEO of Bombardier International, for providing us with our initial inspiration and for supporting our early research on the Millennium Round.

We owe a special debt of gratitude to John Curtis of the Department of Foreign Affairs and International Trade, without whose assistance and support *Seattle and Beyond* could not have been written. John enthusiastically encouraged us and opened many doors for us at the Department. His careful review of an early draft provided us with valuable ideas and allowed us to avoid many errors.

We also thank our friends at Thomas & Davis who supplied us with both encouragement and useful insight. Greg Tereposky in particular attacked our draft with great enthusiasm and provided us with extensive and insightful comments. We also appreciate Kirsten Goodwin's interest and worthwhile suggestions.

In addition, we are grateful to John Sargent who reviewed our chapter "Greening the Rules" and cleared up several difficult points on hazy environmental questions.

We emphasize that the individuals thanked, who were so generous of their time in reviewing our draft, share none of the blame for errors we have stubbornly retained or foolishly introduced after their careful reading and are not responsible for any of the views expressed.

Many other people were also generous with their time and ideas as we worked on the Millennium Round. They include, from DFAIT, Jonathan Fried, John Klassen, David Devine, Susan Sheehan, Tim Miller and Gerald Snyder; from Industry Canada, Nelson Guillemette; from the BCNI, Stewart Carr; and from the Canadian Chamber of Commerce, David Hecnar and Bob Keyes.

We are grateful to Jeff Danziger of the *Los Angeles Times,* Anthony Jenkins of the *Globe and Mail,* Stuart Carlson of the Universal Press Syndicate, and Clay Bennett for permission to reprint their germane cartoons.

In addition to all those that helped us, we also owe a debt of gratitude to the WTO for its excellent world wide web site (www.wto.org) which provided us with the motherlode of information to mine for this book.

List of Acronyms

AA	Agreement on Agriculture
AB	Appellate Body
ACP	Africa, Caribbean and Pacific
APEC	Asia-Pacific Economic Co-operation Forum
ASEAN	Association of South East Asian Nations
ATC	Agreement on Textiles and Clothing
CAP	Common Agricultural Policy
CITES	Convention on International Trade in Endangered Species
CRTA	Australia-New Zealand Closer Relations Trade Area
CRTC	Canadian Radio-Television and Telecommunications Commission
EU	European Union
DSU	Dispute Settlement Understanding
EPZ	Export Processing Zone
EFTA	European Free Trade Area
EVSL	APEC's Early Voluntary Sectoral Liberalization
FDI	Foreign Direct Investment
FTA	Canada-US Free Trade Agreement
FTAA	Free Trade Agreement of the Americas
GATS	General Agreement on Trade in Services
GATT	General Agreement on Tariffs and Trade
GDP	Gross Domestic Product
GPA	Agreement on Government Procurement
GSP	Generalized System of Preferences
ILO	International Labour Organization
IMF	International Monetary Fund
IP	Intellectual Property
ITA	Information Technology Agreement
MAI	Multilateral Agreement on Investment
MEA	Multilateral Environment Agreement
Mercosur	Southern Cone Common Market (Argentina, Brazil, Paraguay and Uruguay)

MFA	Multi-Fibre Arrangement
MFN	Most Favoured Nation
NAFTA	North American Free Trade Agreement
NGOs	Non-Governmental Organizations
NTB	Non-Tariff Barrier
OECD	Organization for Economic Co-operation and Development
PPM	Process and Production Methods
QR	Quantitative Restriction
Quad	US, EU, Japan and Canada
RIA	Regional Integration Agreement
SAGIT	Sectoral Advisory Group on International Trade
SCM	Subsidies and Countervailing Measures
SPS	Sanitary and Phytosanitary
TBT	Technical Barriers to Trade
TPC	Technology Partnerships Canada
TPRM	Trade Policy Review Mechanism
TREMs	Trade-Related Environmental Measures
TRIMs	Trade-Related Investment Measures
TRIPs	Trade-Related Aspects of Intellectual Property Rights
UNEP	United Nations Environment Programme
USTR	United States Trade Representative
WTO	World Trade Organization

Introduction

In early December, the Millennium Round of multilateral trade negotiations will be launched in Seattle. Judging from the statements emanating from the capitals of the world, the round will be comprehensive, covering industrial goods as well as agriculture and services. It will go on for at least three years, but probably longer, and will be the first test of the new World Trade Organization (WTO) under the leadership of its new Director General, Michael Moore. The WTO was established in 1995 following the Uruguay Round to provide an institutional home for the complicated web of trade agreements that had grown up around the General Agreement on Tariffs and Trade (GATT). The Millennium Round will provide a real opportunity to begin the new century with an expanded and strengthened rules-based world trading system. With a successful start, the 21st century could eventually come to be known as the time when global free trade became a reality.

The Millennium Round will not be easy. Technically, it will involve new and complicated issues that will have to be debated and resolved. The new issues include e-commerce, competition policy, the environment and labour standards. Further work also needs to be done on the issues that were new in the last round such as trade in services and intellectual property rights. And then there is trade in agriculture, which is still badly in need of reform after a modest start in the last round.

Politically, the round will be very controversial from the start and face very strong opposition. In addition to the usual resistance from business and agriculture groups that benefit from protection and stand to lose the most from liberalization, there is the new public interest opposition from national, labour and environmental groups that is less obviously based in raw self interest. For some of these public interest groups, the WTO has come to be regarded as a symbol of all that is wrong with the world – the erosion of national sovereignty by globalization, the degradation of the environment by multinational corporations, unsafe genetically modified foods, and job losses and wage cuts blamed on low-wage foreign competition. These public interest groups don't acknowledge the increased output and improvement in living standards produced by freer international trade. They ignore the opportunities to better protect the environment and support society's most vulnerable members that are made possible by the increased income generated through trade.

The Multilateral Agreement on Investment (MAI), which was recently abandoned by governments intimidated by misguided opposition from public interest groups, provides a good example of what can happen when economists and trade specialists don't participate as prominently in the public debate. The case against the MAI was not soundly based in economics, but played on the public's fears and ignorance. There is a real risk that the same thing could happen in Millennium Round. But the stakes are higher this time. A failure of the Millennium Round would badly damage the WTO and threaten the world trading system.

It's important to the success of the Millennium Round that the public be given complete and accurate information on the issues and understand fully how the world trading system works and can be improved. *Seattle and Beyond: The WTO Millennium Round* is our contribution to improving the public's understanding and appreciation of trade issues. It is intended to serve as a guide to all those concerned about the WTO and the issues faced in the Millennium Round. We hope that our readership will include interested laypeople and businesspeople as well as economists, lawyers and trade policy practitioners.

Seattle and Beyond

Chapter 1

The Stakes in Seattle

TRADE NEGOTIATORS MEET PROTESTORS

The Third WTO Ministerial Meeting, which is scheduled to be held in Seattle, Washington from November 30 to December 3, 1999, certainly won't be a quiet, dignified affair as in the early GATT rounds. In those good old days, small chummy groups of trade negotiators used to meet in a stately chateau in Geneva to drink tea and cut deals. This time when trade ministers and officials gather behind the closed doors of the Washington State Trade and Convention Center to go about the important, but unexciting, business of setting the agenda for a new Millennium Round of multilateral trade negotiations, a rainbow coalition of protestors will be massing outside to demonstrate against globalization. And among them will be a core of elite activists, shock troops trained at a nearby boot camp in the latest guerilla protest manoeuvres like scaling buildings and blocking traffic. Outnumbered as well as outyelled, the 5,000 official delegates from 150 countries in attendance may experience some sleeplessness in Seattle.

The anti-trade protestors will make for much more colourful TV than what is going on inside. And as usual they will probably get most of the air time to express their specious arguments and gut opposition to freer trade. That's too bad because the public deserves to hear more about the benefits of trade and the key role the WTO plays in the world trading system. It also needs to hear some concrete ideas about what can be done to improve the system. Nihilism may be more fun, but it is not very constructive.

The demonstrations in Seattle will be far from spontaneous. Planning has been underway for months. The Seattle City Council helped set the stage by voting unanimously to make the city an "MAI-Free Zone." Mike Dolan, the field director of Global Trade Watch, an offshoot of Ralph Nader's Public Citizen group, has spent much time in Seattle and elsewhere mobilizing opposition to the WTO. Environmental groups like Greenpeace, the Friends of the Earth and the Sierra Club are planning to be in Seattle to make sure that their views about the environmental havoc wreaked by trade gets plenty of press. Labour groups, such as the US steelworkers and longshoremen, will also be there to demonstrate against the harm that trade does to the workers of the world regardless of whether they come from developed or developing countries. Who knows? Canada's own Maude Barlow may even put in an appearance in Seattle.

And if it wasn't already hard enough to stand up to the opponents of the WTO who claimed that it is in the pocket of big corporations, the Seattle host committee chaired by Bill Gates of Microsoft and Phil Condit of Boeing had to embark on a campaign of creative financing for the conference, the first WTO meeting ever to be paid for by the private sector. In its letters to corporate donors seeking money to pay for the Conference, the committee offered what looked very much like access to participating trade ministers and officials. Even though the committee modified its letters when the US Government complained, the spot of influence peddling will not be so easy to get out.

Trade and globalization has become very hot of late. And the opponents of trade have tasted blood with their success in getting the industrialized countries to scrap the proposed Multilateral Agreement on Investment (MAI), which they claimed put corporations ahead of people. Perceiving the vulnerability of the fledgling WTO, the anti-traders are anxious to push their advantage and to take on the WTO now when public support appears weak.

Governments, particularly in North America and Europe, were badly stung by the apparent success of non-governmental organizations in stirring up opposition to the MAI. A new euphemism – "civil society" – is used to refer to these groups. "Managing the relationship with civil society" has become a preoccupation of governments in the industrialized world. Some would even say an obsession to the exclusion of providing leadership for the new trade round.

As the Millennium Round gets underway, there will be many complicated and sensitive issues on the table, just as there were in the failed MAI negotiations. Unfortunately, unless economists take a much larger role in the public debate than they have, the public's understanding of the issues will be distorted by the simplistic and illogical views voiced by the outspoken opponents of freer trade. Practitioners of the dismal science may not agree on many things, but, since Adam Smith and David Ricardo, the one thing they do agree on is that free trade improves economic welfare. Comparative advantage and the potential gains from trade is as close to a scientific theory as one gets in the social sciences.

Much is at stake in Seattle and particularly its aftermath. The Millennium Round will be an important symbol of the direction that world trade is going to take in the 21st century. Either there will be continued progress towards an integrated global economy or a back-slide into growing protectionism and uncertainty. Trade dynamics is peculiar that way. It can't stand still. It either moves forward or it falls back, kind of like pushing a car up a hill.

Because there is so much at stake and so little understanding of the issues, we felt compelled to write this book. It's intended to provide a straightforward presentation of the key issues likely to arise in the Millennium Round from an economic perspective. Hopefully, this will be useful in clearing up some of the misconceptions that are likely to arise when the loudest voices providing information on difficult economic issues are coming from those who know diddlysquat about economics.

We provide, in this chapter, an overview of the stakes and issues of the Millennium Round. In subsequent chapters we deal with particular issues in more depth. A final chapter offers our concluding views on where the trade round is headed.

THE GAINS FROM EXPANDED TRADE

Expanding trade is very important for the continued prosperity of the global economy. It enables countries with small internal markets, like Canada, the opportunity to take advantage of the economies of scale and scope that the larger international market offers. This generates increases in productivity and rises in living standards.

Rapidly growing world trade, spurred by tariff cuts and the removal of quantitative barriers over the course of eight rounds of multilateral trade negotiations, has been the main engine driving the global economy since the Second World War. Tariffs of industrialized countries were slashed from high-double-digit rates right after the war, to less than 10 per cent in the 1960s, and to less than 4 per cent today. Over the last three rounds, tariff reductions have averaged a hefty 35 per cent.

Trade has outpaced output growth by a substantial margin since the war, accounting for a growing share of output and employment. From 1948 to 1997, trade grew 6 per cent per year, while output rose only 3.7 per cent per year. Over this period, trade mushroomed a spectacular seventeen-fold, while output increased a more modest, but still hefty, six-fold. By 1997 world exports had reached a whopping US$5.3 trillion.

The WTO estimated that the Uruguay Round results alone would boost world trade volumes by 6 to 20 per cent and raise world income by US$200-

500 billion per year. The Canadian Department of Finance estimated the Canadian share of the gains to be CAN\$3 billion annually. No small potatoes.

A widely cited study by Jeffrey Sachs and Andrew Warner of Harvard University found that countries that were open to trade tended to grow much more rapidly than those that weren't. Over the 1970s and 1980s, developed open economies grew 2.3 per cent per year and closed ones 0.7 per cent; developing open economies grew 4.5 per cent per year and closed ones only 0.7 per cent.

Trade creates jobs as well as growth in output. Canada is a good example of the beneficial effects of trade expansion on job creation. While the Canadian Government was relatively modest, only claiming that 120 thousand new jobs would result from the Canada-U.S Free Trade Agreement, employment increased 1.5 million or 11.8 per cent in the ten years following its 1989 implementation. Much of this can be attributed to the doubling in real exports, which took place over this period. Without the spectacular export growth, the Canadian economy would have experienced very high unemployment because domestic demand growth was weak.

Trade also lowers the prices that consumers pay for good and services and widens their choices. Most recently, the Uruguay Round liberalized the trade restrictions on textiles and clothing imposed under the Multi-Fibre Arrangement. This has already resulted in significant reductions in clothing prices in many industrialized countries. The prices of other goods have also been reduced or increased less as a result of the Uruguay Round tariff cuts, but because the impact was small this has been less evident. However, over the whole period since the Second World War, the price reductions have been much more substantial reflecting the magnitude of the overall tariff decreases.

THE WTO

The World Trade Organization, the focus of the controversy and consequently of this book, is the member-directed institution administering the rules governing world trade. It was created in 1995 as the result of a Canadian Uruguay Round initiative. The General Agreement on Tariffs and Trade (GATT) had finally been given an institutional home, completing the Bretton Woods troika of international institutions. The original American proposal made after the Second World War to create an International Trade Organization to go along with the International Monetary Fund and World Bank had been dropped in the face Congressional opposition. The world trading system had had to limp along without proper institutional support for almost fifty years because of this unfortunate political retreat.

Over a series of eight rounds of trade negotiations under the GATT, a complex web of some 60 agreements governing world trade grew up. It has now been integrated as part of the Uruguay Round outcome and placed under the WTO. An updated GATT with annexes covering specific sectors such as agriculture and textiles, and specific issues such as state trading, product standards, subsidies and anti-dumping, has become the umbrella agreement mandating non-discrimination for trade in goods. A General Agreement on Trade in Services (GATS), which contains both a framework and specific commitments for opening up service sectors to international competition, does the same for services. An Agreement on Trade-Related Aspects of Intellectual Property Rights (TRIPs) provides protection to "intellectual property" such as patents, copyrights, trademarks, and trade secrets when trade is involved. Finally, a strengthened Dispute Settlement Understanding establishes procedures for resolving trade disputes without resort to unilateral actions. There are now 135 countries that are Members of the WTO and bound by these agreements. The number is growing all the time with important countries like China, Russia, Saudi Arabia, and Taiwan negotiating to get in and Georgia completing the final formalities required for admittance.

The importance of the WTO to the world economy is all out of proportion to its relatively modest budget of only 124.8 million Swiss Francs in 1999 (a Swiss Franc equals about 96 cents Canadian). While this may seem like a lot of money, it's not much for an international institution. The IMF spends that much on travel alone.

Canada is a middle-sized country that is heavily dependent on international trade. Exports account for more than 40 per cent of GDP and one job in three is export related. While it's true that the lion's share of this trade is with the United States and is governed by the North American Free Trade Agreement (NAFTA), the WTO Agreements also apply and in some cases cover areas largely untouched by NAFTA such as agriculture. Canada has much to gain from a Millennium Round that will extend and strengthen the WTO and its rules-based trading system. By the same token, Canada has much to lose from any weakening of the WTO which would jeopardize our future economic security. The larger entities like the United States and the European Union are more secure in their large internal markets and have less at stake. A strengthened world trading system would enable Canada to take advantage of growth opportunities in other parts of the world and thereby diversify its exports, almost 85 per cent of which currently go to the United States.

THE AGENDA

Some may ask, "Why another round of multilateral trade negotiations right now? Didn't we just get through the Uruguay Round?" While it may feel like the Uruguay Round just finished, given that it involved so many difficult negotiations and took eight years, it was actually formally concluded in Marrakesh, Morocco on April 15, 1994, and has now been over for more than a half a decade. A trade regime like any other mechanism, even with regular maintenance and tuning, can still use a major overhaul every five years or so. There have been major changes in computers and telecommunications that have fundamentally altered business practices and government administration since the agenda was set for the Uruguay Round. The participation of developing countries, which are coming under the full disciplines of the WTO system according to the timetable set in the Uruguay Round, needs to be enhanced. Moreover, the WTO itself is a new institution and its experience has provided many valuable lessons for institutional reform.

In addition, there was already an agreed built-in agenda for trade negotiations left over from the Uruguay Round in agriculture (AA Article 20), services (negotiations of more specific commitments under GATS Articles XIX and of disciplines for subsidies under GATS Article XV), intellectual property (TRIPs Articles 65 and 71), government procurement (GPA Article XXVII:7), and other matters. This means that even without a new overall round, negotiations will have to get underway soon in some of the most controversial sectors. These negotiations would be rendered much more difficult if the negotiating agenda were not expanded to enable the broader trade-offs that are necessary to make sure that every WTO Member comes out an overall winner.

In a speech before the WTO in Geneva in May 1998, President Clinton called for a new round of global trade talks to be launched in a ministerial meeting to be held in the United States. His speech was so successful that it almost ended up getting the round named after him. But the name suggested by Sir Leon Brittain, the former EU Trade Commissioner, appears to be the one that will stick, that is unless trade ministers decide to christen it the Seattle Round. Since President Clinton's speech, a consensus has developed on the need for a Millennium Round amongst the membership of the WTO. In early May 1999, the Quad trade group consisting of the US, EU, Japan and Canada agreed to support, at a minimum in addition to agriculture and services, negotiations on tariff cuts for industrial goods in the next round of WTO talks. In late May 1999, OECD trade and finance ministers said that the new round of trade talks should have "an ambitious, broad-based and balanced agenda." At the close of their June meeting, the trade ministers of the Asia Pacific Economic Cooperation forum, which has 21 Pacific Rim countries as members including the United States, Japan, China, and Canada, also endorsed a broad round of trade talks. While leaving open the issue of the precise scope of the negotiations, the developing country opposition to a comprehensive new round seems to have been transformed into resignation, even though some developing countries such as Malaysia still claim they're not yet ready to start another round.

There are many issues that could legitimately be included on the negotiating table in the Millennium Round. These are summarized here and will be treated in greater detail in the chapters of this book:

- *Tariff Reductions* Even after eight rounds, tariffs are still high on many industrial goods (tariff "spikes") and in many, particularly developing, countries. In the Bogar Declaration of November 1994, APEC leaders called for an elimination of tariffs by its industrialized members by 2010 and by its developing members by 2020. The First Summit of the Americas in Miami in December 1994 called for the conclusion of a Free Trade Agreement of the Americas (FTAA) by 2005. The WTO could make a commitment similar to these two and seek to make significant progress towards its attainment in the next round.

- *Non-Tariff Barriers*   With lower tariffs, non-tariff barriers become more important in limiting market access. There are technical issues in the areas of standards, rules of origin and customs valuation that need to be resolved. The Agreement on Technical Barriers to Trade, the Agreement on Rules of Origin, and the Valuation Agreement could be improved.

- *Regional Trade Agreements* There has been a proliferation of regional free trade agreements in recent years. These include most notably the NAFTA, the EU in Europe, and Mercosur in South America. These agreements are beneficial as long as they are trade creating rather than trade diverting. But more recent bilateral free trade agreements between the EU and the countries of Eastern Europe and North Africa, and the proposed FTAA have the potential to distort trade because the less developed partners retain high tariffs on imports from the rest of the world.

- *Agriculture* Progress was made in the Uruguay Round in reducing domestic subsidies, curbing export subsidies, and replacing non-tariff measures with bound tariffs that can be transparently phased out over time. However, substantial domestic and export subsidies still exist, particularly under the EU Common Agricultural Policy (CAP). Moreover, the process of tariffication has resulted in bound over-quota tariffs at such high levels that very little trade has developed. Importing dairy products to Canada where over-quota dairy tariff rates are 200 or even 300 per cent on some products is a good case in point. Even where in-quota access is available under low or nominal tariffs, such access is minimal. Finally, state trading enterprises have played a role in limiting competition and influencing both export and import prices of agricultural products falling within their jurisdiction. Much more must be done to eliminate export and trade distorting domestic subsidies and truly to liberalize trade in agriculture. But key WTO Members such as the EU, Japan and Korea will continue to fight liberalization tooth and nail. In addition to trade liberalization, other difficult issues – touching consumers directly – include trade in genetically modified organisms and the application of sanitary and phyto-sanitary regulations, the latter exemplified by the recent dispute where the US and Canada squared off against the EU over hormone-treated beef. Notwithstanding internal political sensitivities over the fate of supply-managed sectors and the Canadian Wheat Board, Canada has a huge stake in liberalized trade in agriculture. This is particularly true for our red meat and grains producers and exporters of agri-food products.

• *Services* Progress has been made in reaching agreements in such new economy services as financial services and basic telecommunications since the conclusion of the Uruguay Round. Negotiations on many important issues such as labour mobility, air and sea transportation services, and subsidies have yet to be undertaken. National treatment for market access needs to be expanded to cover a much broader range of services and more modes of supply than those currently listed in each Member's schedules of commitments. National and most-favoured-nation (MFN) treatment, the two fundamental obligations of non-discrimination of the GATT, should also become the rule for services rather than the exception.

• *Government Procurement* The numerous exceptions to the principle of non-discrimination in the Agreement on Government Procurement (GPA) need to be further circumscribed. The coverage needs to be extended to cover non-federal levels of government procurement. This is a particularly sensitive issue for Canada, which cannot gain access to procurement opportunities in other countries' non-federal sectors because many of the provincial governments refuse to allow their own procurement to be covered. The membership in the plurilateral GPA needs to be expanded beyond the 26 countries that are currently parties. An Agreement on Transparency in Government Procurement, which is being developed, needs to be accepted by all WTO Members. Government procurement of services needs to be included in the GATS.

- *Electronic Commerce* With the success of companies like Amazon.com and Dell computer, e-commerce is likely to become increasingly important. The US Trade Representative estimates that it should grow in the US from $8 billion last year to $327 billion in 2002. Not only does e-commerce promise to change the way we do business, but it also interferes with governments' ability to tax and regulate commercial transactions. Inevitably, some international rules will be required and the WTO is the preferred forum for their development. At the insistence of the United States, there has been a moratorium on tariffs on e-commerce since 1998. However, it only applies to goods and services like software and accounting that are delivered electronically, and not to goods that are ordered on the Internet but physically delivered across borders. Other countries are concerned about US dominance of the Internet and may push for restrictions. There are also concerns about consumer protection and privacy.
- *Antidumping, Subsidies and Countervailing Measures* The increased reliance on antidumping, and countervailing duties is an unanticipated outcome of the Uruguay Round. These measures need to be better disciplined by WTO rules to prevent abuse. There is also a need to consider how best to discipline subsidies granted to services and service suppliers.
- *Investment* Foreign investment and trade have become increasingly linked. Aside from the rather modest provisions of the TRIPs Agreement and the commercial presence provisions in the GATS, there are few concrete rules governing investment in foreign markets. Businesses in developed countries are calling for measures to prevent discrimination in the establishment and operation of investment, protect the property rights of investors, and provide guarantees against confiscation or other tantamount government measures. Such rules would help to promote investment and generate growth in the countries attracting the investment. Competition policy is also important to make sure that foreign investors have access to all sectors and that foreign firms can compete on an equal basis with domestic. There is also a need to do something to prevent countries from using financial incentives to lure investment away from other countries. With the demise of the MAI, it is now up to the WTO to develop rules for investment on a more inclusive global basis.
- *Extraterritoriality* The extraterritorial application of one country's laws to another is a hot topic at the WTO. The worst offender is the US with its Helms-Burton Act and Iran-Libya Sanctions Act. Canada and the European Union have both been subject to sanctions for trading or investing in Cuba. Sherritt International's Ian Delaney is banned from entering the

United States. The EU has threatened to take the US to the WTO over Helms-Burton, but backed off when the US claimed a national security exemption. It will be hard to keep this issue off the table in the Millennium Round, but the United States will certainly try.

- *Intellectual Property* This will continue to be an important issue for the upcoming round. The United States will be pushing for greater protection of intellectual property in their strong sectors such as entertainment software, computer software, and pharmaceuticals. The US is certain to encounter resistence from other nations, including some of their counterparts in the developed world. Developing countries, which have not been fully able to implement all their commitments under the existing TRIPs Agreement, will be the greatest source of resistance.

- *Culture* Culture is not covered explicitly by the WTO agreements. The United States is most aggressive in attacking barriers to the export of its cultural products including television shows, movies, music, magazines and books. Other countries led by France and Canada seek to preserve their ability to protect culture from foreign influences. Canada recently lost a WTO challenge on split-run magazines (i.e. magazines with primarily foreign editorial content, but with advertising directed to Canadians). Under pressure from the United States, a negotiated settlement was reached that gave US magazines access to Canadian advertising revenue subject to certain limits. Early rumblings suggest that the issue of the treatment of cultural products will be a highly explosive one in the upcoming round.

- *Environment* Environmental regulation is another very sensitive area of unfinished business for the upcoming round. The nexus between environmental and trade policy is extremely nebulous and puts much strain on negotiators and legislators. The perception that the WTO trade agreements threaten the environment by preventing the enforcement of legitimate environmental measures has been fostered by the well-known Dolphin-Tuna, the Shrimp-Turtle, and Gasoline Standards cases where panels ruled against the United States. While current WTO provisions permit environmental measures necessary to protect human, animal or plant life or health (GATT Article XX) provided there are no alternative GATT-consistent or less GATT-inconsistent measure available to achieve the desired objectives, better rules governing the interplay between trade and environmental regulations are needed to strengthen the world trading system. Without them, it will be difficult to get the required support in North American and Europe for other Millennium Round initiatives.

- *Labour Standards* Much of the opposition to liberalized trade stems from a fear that jobs will be lost to imports from countries where workers are paid low wages and where labour operates under substandard conditions. There is also some genuine, but misguided, concern that the conditions of workers in these low wage countries will be exacerbated by liberalized trade under the WTO. These concerns led to a labour side-agreement under NAFTA, which was carefully crafted to avoid setting standards and to prevent standards issues from going to dispute settlement. There will be pressure to address the issue of labour standards in the context of trade in the upcoming round. One suggestion is for a greater role for the International Labour Organization (ILO) in setting minimally acceptable standards in cooperation with the WTO. It's clear that something will have to be done in this round to satisfy the United States and Europe. But it is also evident that whatever is done will have to be acceptable to developing countries and not compromise their comparative advantage in labour-intensive goods.

- *Dispute Settlement Mechanism* One of the biggest achievements of the Uruguay Round was the establishment of the WTO Dispute Settlement Understanding (DSU). It allows independent panels to decide cases put before them on a more timely and definitive basis than under the old GATT. Unlike in the past, WTO panel decisions are now binding on Members unless overturned by the Appellate Body on appeal. Nevertheless, some weaknesses in the process have been identified. In particular, there is a need for: more clarity in implementing panel decisions; greater openness and transparency in the process; opportunities for private sector participation; and less delay in releasing panel decisions.

- *Accession* The rules-based international trading system should be extended to cover all economies as quickly as practicable. Thirty countries and customs territories have applied to join the WTO. China, Chinese Taipei (Taiwan), Russia, Saudi Arabia, Ukraine, Estonia, Lithuania, and Vietnam are among the 20 applicants with which active negotiations are proceeding. The most important of these are China, Russia, Saudi Arabia, and Taiwan. China almost reached agreement with the Americans during Premier Zhu Rongji's visit to the US in April, but the May 7th bombing of the Chinese Embassy in Belgrade and the release of the Congressional report on nuclear espionage knocked the accession negotiations badly off track. It's important to bring China and Russia into the WTO club as soon as possible so that they can be full participants in the international trading system, including during the Millennium Round.

THE PROCESS

Economic purists think the whole process of trade negotiations smacks of mercantilism. This is an outdated economic theory, much berated by Adam Smith and David Ricardo, that encouraged export and discouraged imports so as to accumulate gold bullion, which the mercantilists erroneously regarded to be the source of a country's wealth. Similarly, the basic premise behind the eight rounds of multilateral trade negotiations since the war is that a country should try to get its trading partners to reduce their tariffs and non-tariff barriers (NTBs) on its exports as much as possible, while at the same time reducing its own as little as it can get away with. This flies in the face of the economic objective of maximizing consumer welfare, which would be furthered not only by reductions in foreign tariffs and NTBs but even by a unilateral reduction in tariffs and NTBs. A pragmatic justification of the real-world process of trade negotiations is that reductions in foreign tariffs and NTBs can only be secured by bargaining away domestic tariffs and NTBs. The end result is not only that a country gets foreign tariffs and NTBs down but its own as well. The validity of this justification has been demonstrated by the success of successive rounds of multilateral trade negotiations in bringing down tariffs and eliminating NTBs. It's hard to argue against success.

Concerning the exact nature of the process, there are different views on how best to structure the negotiations -- single-undertaking versus sector-by-sector or sector clusters. Single-undertaking is the most comprehensive approach. Under it, nothing is settled until everything is settled. Previously agreed issues can be reopened at any time until all the issues are resolved. This is the way the Uruguay Round worked. It enables the parties to the negotiation to have the maximum flexibility in terms of trade-offs amongst the issues. The downside is that a single-undertaking negotiation can be difficult to bring to a conclusion and can take a long time to complete. That's why US Trade Representative Charlene Barshefsky said, "We absolutely will not sign on the notion of a single-undertaking if that means every issue and the kitchen sink has to be decided before the core issues of market access are decided for the round to conclude."

In contrast, sector-by-sector is a piecemeal approach. Under it, the parties reach binding agreements on each individual sector (or issue) and the whole round is complete when all the sectors are settled. There is no going back to reopen settled sectors if the parties are dissatisfied with the offers on subsequent sectors. It may be easier to bring a sector-by-sector negotiation to completion if it is possible to segment all the issues into nice compartmentalized sectors on which agreement can be easily reached. At the September APEC meeting in Auckland, the United States was pushing a sectoral approach, but ran into heavy resistance from Japan which is defensive about its agriculture, forestry and fisheries sectors.

Intermediate in comprehensiveness between single-undertaking and sector-by-sector is the cluster approach, which was proposed by former Canadian Trade Minister and now Canadian WTO Ambassador Sergio Marchi. It would group the sectors together into broad enough clusters to allow meaningful trade-offs. It may make it easier to reach agreement, but only if the right clusters are created. This may be harder than it sounds.

Originally, the EU and Japan favoured single-undertaking and the United States a sector-by-sector approach. But a consensus seems to be emerging in favour of a single-undertaking approach as long as the package is kept "manageable," to use the term employed by the US Trade Representative. But since what is "manageable" tends to grow because it must include what everyone wants, this probably means another Uruguay-like round is probably in store.

There is the possibility of an "early harvest" of agreements on some issues at Seattle before a new round is launched. These issues include electronic commerce and transparency in government procurement.

THE TIMETABLE

The Uruguay Round was launched in Punta del Esta, Uruguay in September 1986 and didn't finally conclude until April 15, 1994 in Marrakesh, Morocco, almost eight years later. There is almost universal agreement among WTO Members that this is an unacceptably long period for a trade negotiation to take even on the basis of a single-undertaking approach. As one wag put it, "They call it the Millennium Round because of when it starts, not because of how long it is supposed to take."

The APEC trade ministers and OECD trade and finance ministers have agreed to a three-year target for the negotiations. This will probably be accepted at the Seattle Ministerial as the time frame for the Millennium Round. But it's one thing to set a deadline and another to meet it. So it is always possible that an agreement won't be reached before the deadline. The Uruguay Round had several such deadlines that were passed unmet. Nevertheless, if three years is accepted as the target, it's certainly unlikely that the negotiations will be allowed to drag on as long as the Uruguay Round negotiations. In addition, this time the WTO provides an institutional setting that is more conducive to "rolling," continuous negotiations. If some issues aren't resolved by the end of the three years or shortly thereafter, it will always be possible to mandate an ongoing work program in particular areas and to call an end to the round.

OBSTACLES

There are many obstacles that will have to be overcome to complete a successful Millennium Round. In the first place, it will not be easy to get the process smoothly underway. The difficulty in choosing a new Director General of the WTO does not augur well for the ability of member countries to come up with common agenda. Decisions in the WTO are made by consensus. This worked all right in narrowing down the number of candidates from four to two, but then a deadlock developed that left the WTO headless for six months. The United States backed Michael Moore, the former New Zealand Prime Minister and Trade Minister, and an Asian block led by Japan stood firmly behind Supachai Panitchpakdi, the Thai Deputy Prime Minister. Both sides refused to budge. The only way that a compromise could finally be reached was to split, Solomon-like, a six-year term by making Moore the Director General for a three-year term beginning in September to be followed by Supachai for the next three years. This unorthodox arrangement, with Moore finishing his term before the completion of the Millennium Round, will make it more difficult to bring the negotiations to a timely and satisfactory conclusion. It also underlines the great difficulty of making hard decisions by consensus in the WTO.

Decision-making at the WTO will also be hampered by an emerging conflict between the Quad group (the United States, Europe, Japan, and Canada) that support further trade liberalization and developing countries that are much less enthusiastic. In past rounds, this was not a problem as the Quad always dominated multilateral negotiations.

The forces of protectionism, which are on the rise particularly in the United States, are another major obstacle. Large increases in US steel imports from Japan, South Korea, Russia and Brazil set off alarm bells last year. Consequently, steel quota bills are currently before the United States Congress and an accord limiting steel exports was reached between the United States and Russia in July. The United States has also been aggressive in extending the coverage of products under the Canada-US softwood lumber agreement, which voluntarily restricts exports. Trade disputes between the US and Europe over bananas and hormone-treated beef could also lead to further protectionist or retaliatory measures.

The US Government also lacks fast-track authority which is necessary for the US Administration to conclude a trade negotiation. Without fast-track, the trade legislation implementing the ultimate results of the Millennium Round agreement would be subject to amendment in the US Congress. This could put the Administration in the impossible position of having to try to reopen any Millennium Round agreement to incorporate any changes enacted by the Congress. Other countries are unlikely to come to an agreement on these terms.

The 1998 bill providing fast-track authority was blocked by anti-trade Democrats, giving the President a slap in the face from his own party. While fast-track authority may not be necessary to begin a trade negotiation, it is certainly necessary to conclude it. In other trade rounds, the Congressional authorization has lagged the start of negotiations. For the Tokyo Round, it was fifteen months after the round started before the fast-track legislation was passed; for the Uruguay Round, it was two years. In both these cases, the negotiators didn't really get down to brass tacks until the Administration finally got its mandate in the form of the necessary fast-track authority.

Chapter 2

Opening Markets More

TARIFFS

Improved market access for goods, including in particular reduced tariffs, has been the main objective of the General Agreement on Tariffs and Trade ever since it was concluded in 1947. Over eight rounds of multilateral trade negotiations, great progress has been made in lowering average tariff rates on manufactured goods levied by industrialized countries from 40 per cent before GATT to around 4 per cent today. Progress was also made in eliminating other barriers to trade such as exchange controls, import licensing and quotas that were even more damaging to trade than tariffs.

The GATT applied an easy three-step recipe to reduce the overall level of protectionism in the world economy. First, less visible non-tariff trade barriers were, wherever possible, replaced with tariffs or, better still, eliminated. Second, maximum (or "bound") tariff rates were negotiated. Third, the bound rates were lowered further over time in subsequent rounds of negotiations.

For most industrialized countries, bound tariff rates are the same as MFN tariff rates. But for developing countries, bound tariff rates are often much higher than applied rates and serve as a ceiling. This gives these countries the flexibility to raise tariffs arbitrarily and unexpectedly if they so choose. In contrast, countries that bind their tariffs at applied levels must compensate their trading partners if, for any reason, they raise their tariffs.

By far the thickest pile of paper produced by the Uruguay Round contains the detailed schedules of bound tariffs by Harmonized System classification for each individual country participating in the negotiations. The Uruguay Round tariff cuts, which will be fully phased in by the year 2000, will average almost 40 per cent and will lower the average tariff on industrial products levied by developed countries from 6.3 per cent to 3.8 per cent. The proportion of the value of these products that will be duty free will rise from 20 per cent to 44 per cent. The proportion facing high tariffs above 15 per cent will fall from 7 per cent to 5 per cent. And the proportion of these tariff lines that are bound will increase from 78 per cent to 99 per cent.

Tariffs applicable on most of Canada's exports to its most important trading partner, the United States, which accounts for approximately 84 per cent of total Canadian exports, are set at zero under NAFTA. The tariff bindings negotiated under the GATT apply to the rest of Canada's trade, more than half of which is with the European Union (5.5 per cent) and Japan (3 per cent), Canada's next most important trading partners.

According to an OECD study, average tariffs will have been reduced substantially when the Uruguay Round cuts are fully phased in, but they will still have some way to go (Chart 1). Among the four Quad countries, tariffs will average in the 4 to 7 per cent range and be higher in the European Union and Canada than in Japan and the United States. Except for Switzerland and Sweden though, bound tariff rates will be significantly higher in other advanced OECD countries averaging from 9 to 25 per cent. And bound tariffs will be even higher still in the developing countries of Mexico and Turkey averaging 35 to 45 per cent. This is representative of bound tariff rates in the developing world. Bound tariff rates are usually much higher than applied rates in developing countries. Applied tariff rates only averaged 14 per cent in Mexico and 10 per cent in Turkey.

It's not only the level of the tariffs that cause intersectoral distortions in production. A high dispersion of tariff rates combined especially with tariff "spikes" can also lead to a misallocation of resources. The same OECD study presents standard deviations for tariff rates as an indicator of dispersion (Chart 2). They are sufficiently high in the OECD's view to be a potential source of distortions. (The extraordinarily high standard deviation of tariff rates in Norway results from the tariffication of agricultural tariff rates.) Tariff "spikes," which are defined as exceeding three times the simple average of MFN tariff rates, are also prevalent in most countries (Chart 3).

CHART 1
SIMPLE AVERAGE OF BOUND TARIFF RATES ON COMPLETION OF URUGUAY ROUND

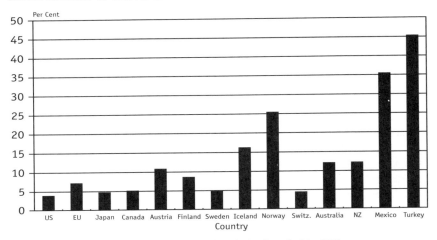

Source: OECD, Indicators of Tariff and Non-tariff Trade Barriers: Update 1997.

CHART 2
OVERALL STANDARD DEVIATION FOR ALL TARIFF RATES IN 1996 AS MEASURED BY
IMPORT COVERAGE RATIO

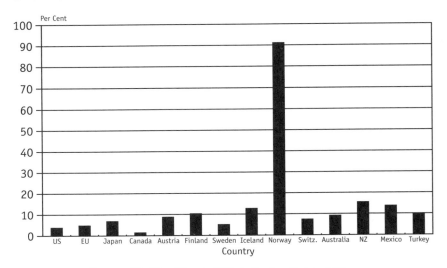

Source: OECD, Indicators of Tariff and Non-tariff Trade Barriers: Update 1997.

CHART 3
TARIFF SPIKES IN 1996

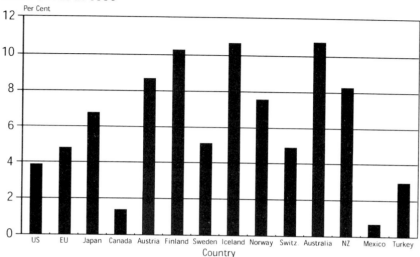

Source: OECD, Indicators of Tariff and Non-tariff Trade Barriers: Update 1997.
Note: Tariff "spikes" are defined as those exceeding 3 times the simple average MFN rate.

A good example of a tariff "spike" occurs in truck tariffs, which are 22 per cent in the European Union and 25 per cent in the United States. The United States has relatively high tariffs for textiles, ceramics and glass, but this doesn't affect Canada because of the NAFTA. Some high tariffs facing Canadian producers include European Union tariffs on fish products (7 to 22 per cent), plywood (6 to 10 per cent), and non-ferrous metals including especially aluminum (7.5 per cent).

Even seemingly low tariffs can provide important protection. The OECD tariff study found a significant degree of tariff "escalation" in some countries. When this occurs, effective tariff protection increases as goods undergo further processing. For example, the Japanese tariff on lumber is only 4.8 per cent, but that's high enough to make it hard for Canadian lumber exporters to compete with Japanese lumber manufacturers who can import raw logs duty free.

In its recent report, the Standing Committee on Foreign Affairs and International trade found that tariffs are still very high in many developing countries not covered by the OECD study. By region, tariffs are highest in South Asia, where they averaged around 45 per cent in the early 1990s. Next comes Africa, where tariffs average in the 25 to 30 per cent range. Tariffs in East Asia (excluding China) and Latin America average in the 10 to 20 per cent range.

A discussion of the extraordinarily high tariffs on many agricultural goods following the Uruguay Round tariffication exercise is reserved for the next chapter on agriculture.

There is clearly lots of room to cut tariffs further in the Millennium Round, even taking into account that they remain an important source of government revenue in many developing and transition economies. An ambitious objective for developed industrialized countries would be to try to reduce tariffs to zero or as close thereto as possible. For developing countries, another round of 30 to 40 per cent reductions would be a reasonable objective.

NON-TARIFF BARRIERS

While much progress has been made in eliminating or lowering non-tariff barriers, they still exist and are important. The OECD study referred to above examined the prevalence of NTBs among OECD countries. The NTBs considered fell under two rubrics: price controls, and quantitative restrictions (QRs). Price controls covered Voluntary Export Restrictions like those used for automobiles and textiles, variable charges, and antidumping and countervailing duties. QRs included non-automatic licensing, export restraints, and other quotas and import prohibitions. The OECD study showed that QRs have not yet been confined to the dustbin of history (Chart 4). Ignoring Austria, QRs were most prevalent among the Quad countries, particularly the European Union and the United States. This suggest that the more advanced the economy the more subtle a form that protectionism assumes.

Chart 4

Importance of Non-Tariff Barriers in 1996 as Measured by Import Coverage Ratio

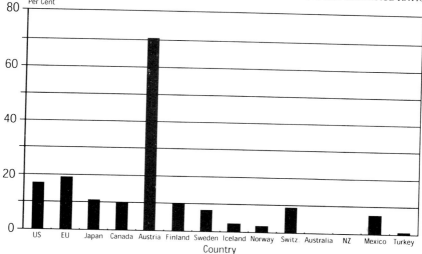

Source: OECD, Indicators of Tariff and Non-tariff Trade Barriers: Update 1997.
Note: For US and Japan is measured as proportion of NTB categories.

Trade Facilitation

Work has been underway at the WTO since the 1996 Singapore Ministerial
looking at the practical problems faced by traders in moving goods across borders. This is to see whether existing WTO trade facilitation obligations such as
the Customs Valuation and Rules of Origin Agreements are working and what
more needs to be done. At a symposium held in 1998, which was attended by
business representatives as well as government, there was an abundance of
complaints about the way excessive red tape, inadequate computerization, lack
of transparency, and failure to cooperate between customs and other government agencies made trading needlessly difficult. With just-in-time inventories
and manufacturing, businesses are becoming increasingly dissatisfied with
bureaucratic delays in getting goods through customs. Proposals have been
advanced by some countries, including the United States and Canada, to
improve existing trade facilitation provisions. This work will continue in the
Millennium Round, perhaps even resulting in an Agreement on Trade Facilitation as well as modifications to existing agreements. More transparent proce-

dures for trade and more efficient customs administration are badly needed and would be welcomed by traders throughout the world.

AUTOMOBILES

The tariff waiver implemented by Canada under the Auto Pact, Canada's preferential trade agreement with the United States for its largest and most important industry accounting for $86-billion in output, has been successfully challenged recently by Japan and the European Union before a WTO panel. They claim that the waiver of Canada's 6.1-per-cent MFN tariff on certain vehicle imports from overseas is unfair and discriminatory because it is only made available for imports by North America's Big Three Auto Companies. These three firms are able to import cars from their subsidiaries or affiliates duty free – Ford from Jaguar and Volvo, Daimler-Chrysler from Mercedes Benz, and GM from Saab. So is Suzuki, which acquired Auto Pact status through its investment in the Cami Automotive assembly plant, a joint venture with GM. This preferential treatment contrasts with that of other importers of competing automobiles such as Honda and Toyota, which also produce cars in Canada, but which must pay the 6.1-per-cent duty on any cars that they import. Japan and Europe in their complaint also challenged the Auto Pact more generally as being inconsistent with several of Canada's WTO obligations. The alleged offending provisions concerned the performance requirements for the value of vehicles assembled in Canada and Canadian content, which are tied to the duty waiver.

The panel's preliminary ruling, which became known in mid-October and will probably be approved by the WTO in January, found that the Auto Pact was inconsistent with several WTO obligations and recommended that it, in effect, be abolished. In particular, it found that the duty waiver granted Auto Pact members was discriminatory and constituted a prohibited export subsidy. To comply, the Canadian Government will have to get rid of the Auto Pact, which can be done by order-in-council. The Canadian Government will also have to either eliminate the 6.1-per-cent MFN tariff, or apply it to all imports at the existing rate.

There are arguments on both sides of the issue. On the one hand, the Big Three will lobby the Government to retain the tariff and apply it to all non-North American imports. They will argue that, since the benefit of continued protection on the cars they produce in North America would outweigh the loss of having to pay the tariff on the relatively few cars they import from outside North America, they would be able to provide more economic activity and employment in Canada if the tariff were retained. This protection would, of course, be mitigated by any reduction in the tariff resulting from the Millennium Round and subsequent trade negotiations. But the tariff would be a chip in these negotiations and could be useful in negotiating tariff cuts by other countries.

On the other hand, the Japanese producers, who obviously want to see the tariff eliminated as soon as possible, will argue that the lower car prices that would result would be in the interest of Canadian consumers. Regardless of which side wins the day, however, it shouldn't have a very big affect on the Canadian automobile industry. Automobiles are produced in Canada today because of the strong competitiveness of the Canadian automobile industry and not because of the tariff and the Auto Pact. And most of the cars are made for export not for the domestic market.

TEXTILES AND CLOTHING

The sector that provides the initial impetus in the industrial development of many developing countries is textiles and clothing. It is labour intensive and makes good use of the low-wage, unskilled labour that they have in abundance. The competitiveness of the textiles and clothing industries in developing countries has long been considered a threat to the established industries of the industrialized countries which necessarily must pay wages and benefits many times higher.

The fear of lost jobs and depressed economies in producing regions if textiles and clothing imports were allowed to replace domestic production gave rise to powerful political pressures for protectionist measures. The Multi-Fibre Arrangement (MFA), which was created in 1974 to manage trade in textiles and clothing with the developing countries, was the institutional response of the developed world to the prospect of soaring Third World textile and clothing imports. It established rules that enabled the importing developed countries to impose quotas based on historical shares in bilateral negotiations with the producing developing countries. It also legitimized the use of quantitative restrictions to deal with import surges. This approach was obviously discriminatory and violated basic GATT principles. However, the developing countries that wanted access to the developed world's textiles and clothing market had little choice but to go along, like it or not. But, it, at least, reduced the uncertainty they faced over market access and gave them a share in the quota rents, rather than leaving all the rents to the importing countries.

Given their visceral opposition to the patent unfairness of the MFA, the most important achievement of the Uruguay Round for many developing countries was the new Agreement on Textiles and Clothing (ATC), which embodied a plan to phase out the quantitative restraints of the MFA. At that time four WTO Members – Canada, the European Union, the United States and Norway – still maintained import restrictions.

Under the ATC, the textile and clothing sector is being returned to normal GATT disciplines over a ten-year transition period ending in 2005. The products covered are yarns, fabrics, made-up textile products, and clothing. The process of integration into the rules of GATT is to be carried out progressively in three stages: in the first stage started on January 1, 1995 at least 16 per cent of products were integrated; in the second stage on January 1, 1998 an additional 17 per cent was integrated; in the third stage on January 1, 2002 another 18 per cent will be integrated; and on January 1, 2005 the remaining products will be integrated. The ATC also contains a programme for liberalizing existing restrictions by increasing existing quota growth rates by a specified percentage. In addition, it provides a special transitional safeguard mechanism to protect against import surges of products that are not under quota but are not yet integrated. A Textiles Monitoring Body has been set up to oversee the implementation of the ATC and make sure that any measures taken respect the rules of the agreement.

While quantitative restrictions are already well on their way to being phased out under the ATC, developing country textile and clothing producing countries won't be completely out of the woods until all the products are integrated and the agreement terminated. There is always a risk that the phase out could be extended or additional restrictions could be imposed. Textile and clothing industry lobbyists in the developed world may be down but they're not out yet. The United States Administration demonstrated this when it gave in to pressure from the American Textile Manufacturers Institute, and sought to extend the application of textile quotas to China for an additional five years in its bilateral accession negotiations with China last April.

FORESTRY AND FISHERIES

There's been an ongoing controversy between the United States and Japan in particular over the forestry and fisheries sectors that could spill over into the Millennium Round. The United States, supported by Canada, became the champion of APEC's Early Voluntary Sectoral Liberalization (EVSL) initiative. Fifteen sectors were identified at the 1997 Leaders' meeting in Vancouver in 1997 for liberalization. Forestry and fisheries were among the nine fast-track sectors for which trade liberalization agreements were to be finalized for the 1998 Leaders' meeting in Kuala Lumpur. When it proved impossible to reach agreements, APEC passed the buck to the WTO.

The Japanese are still strongly opposed to any US efforts to achieve an agreement for early liberalization in forestry or fisheries because of the political sensitivity of these sectors, which are characterized by traditional lifestyles and account for much employment. If the Japanese had their druthers, these sectors would get special treatment like agriculture does under the WTO rules. Barring that, they want them to be part of the overall negotiations. The United States, on the other hand, is adamant on the need for quick progress. As a leading exporter of forestry and fisheries products, Canada's interests coincide with the US on this issue.

Forestry and fisheries are special in that they both involve renewable resources. Fisheries are difficult because the widespread mismanagement of fish stock has lead to their depletion. This mismanagement has been compounded by enormous sectoral subsidies that encourage over-fishing. A World Bank study by Milazzo estimates that global fisheries subsidies are in the US$15 to $20 billion range. Other estimates put the subsidies as high as US$50 billion. To promote conservation of fish stocks, these subsidies need to be curtailed by WTO disciplines.

INFORMATION TECHNOLOGY AGREEMENT

After the conclusion of the Uruguay Round, there was a major breakthrough at the 1996 Singapore Ministerial. An Information Technology Agreement was reached to scrap customs duties on telecommunications equipment, software and semiconductors by the year 2000. This agreement is important because it will make the benefits of the revolution in information technology and infrastructure available to users around the world more rapidly and cheaply. It will thus help to narrow the wide international gaps in the access to information technology, and will raise global productivity. But it was not only altruism that motivated the American trade negotiators that were the main force pushing for the agreement. The United States is the home of the world's leading edge information technology sector that is best placed to take advantage of the increased demand for information products.

The ITA took effect on April 1, 1997 after participants accounting for 90 per cent of the $500 billion world trade in information technology products had signed on to agreement (including some like Chinese Tapei that were not yet WTO Members). The first of four equal agreed reductions in tariffs was implemented on July 1, 1997 and the last will be implemented on January 1, 2000. There are now 48 participants in the agreement including the fifteen EU countries. But all WTO Members benefit from the tariff cuts as they are made on a MFN basis.

Countries Participating in the Information Technology Agreement

Australia	Iceland	Macau	Singapore
Canada	India	Malaysia	Slovak Republic
Chinese Tapei	Indonesia	Mauritius	Switzerland (incl. Liechtenstein)
Czech Republic	Israel	New Zealand	
Costa Rica	Japan	Norway	Thailand
El Salvador	Korea	Panama	Turkey
European Union	Kyrgyz Republic	Phillipines	United States
Estonia	Latvia	Poland	
Hong Kong, China	Lithuania	Romania	

Already one WTO case has involved the ITA indirectly. In 1997, the United States challenged the EUs reclassification of networking equipment from the category of computers to telecommunications equipment, which had tariffs nearly twice as high. The panel supported the United States' claim, but the decision was overturned on appeal. The EU defused the controversy by agreeing to have the disputed equipment covered by the ITA agreement, which means that the offending tariff will be eliminated by January 1, 2000.

Efforts have been underway to expand the scope of the ITA. The first review of the ITA produced a long list of additional information technology products that could be added. Discussions went on through 1998 but no agreement could be reached on expanded coverage for a so called ITA-II. Resistance to further liberalization has been strongest from India and Malaysia. But with the ITA expiring next year, the US Trade Representative Charlene Barshefshy is hopeful that it will be possible to reach agreement on an ITA-II with coverage extended to some 200 new products, accounting for an additional $13 billion in sales and including radar and navigational equipment. This could be one of the early harvests of the Millennium Round.

REGIONAL INTEGRATION AGREEMENTS

Members of the WTO are allowed to enter into preferential customs unions and free trade areas with other countries under certain specified conditions set out in Article XXIV of the GATT. They are also allowed to liberalize trade in services preferentially with specific countries under GATS Article V. The main difference between a customs union and a free trade area is that a customs union has a common external tariff against third countries. It also usually involves a higher level of integration.

Regional Integration Agreements (RIAs) have been proliferating and radically altering the trade landscape. Over the last fifty years, more than 150 such arrangements were notified to the GATT and the WTO. Most of these are still around in one form or another. RIAs have multiplied to such an extent that only a handful of WTO Members aren't members of some regional trade pact or other. Half of international trade now takes place within the framework of RIAs.

The reigning heavyweight RIAs are the European Union and the NAFTA. Other major agreements include the Mercosur, the European Free Trade Area (EFTA), the Australia-New Zealand CRTA, South African Customs Union, and the ASEAN free trade area. Canada has free trade agreements with Chile and Israel and is currently negotiating with the EFTA. The European Union has free trade agreements with Central European countries and trade deals with North Africa and Mercosur. New Zealand just signed a trade pact with Singapore at the APEC meeting in Auckland. The EU has concluded a free trade arrangement with South Africa that takes effect next year, and is currrently negotiating with Mexico. Negotiations are underway for a Free Trade Agreement of the Americas (FTAA). And everyday more talks get underway – New Zealand-Chile, Japan-South Korea, South Korea-Mexico – the list goes on. These RIAs run the course from a regional economic union (the EU) to bilateral free trade agreements.

RIAs can be a step down the path to multilateral free trade if they are a manifestation of a general willingness to open up markets and bring down trade barriers. But they can just as easily go the other way if they're really disguised efforts to stake out markets and discriminate against others.

Concern about the contrasting tendencies for and against freer trade inherent in RIAs has led the WTO to establish some basic conditions that a customs union or free trade agreement must meet to qualify under the GATT. First, the agreement must eliminate all the duties and other restrictive regulations of commerce on "substantially all the trade between the constituent territories in products originating in such territories." Second, the proposed implementation of the customs union or free trade area must be in a reasonable period of time.

Third, the agreements can't raise barriers to trade. This means that, as a general rule, the duties and other regulations can't be made higher or more restrictive. The WTO must be notified of the details of any agreement and has the right to approve or reject it, or to recommend changes.

The process of vetting RIAs was sufficiently controversial in the Uruguay Round that an Understanding on the Interpretation of Article XXIV of the GATT was negotiated to clarify the rules. It is in the interest of all non-members of an RIA that the agreement be trade creating and not diverting. But this is probably too much to ask given that almost all WTO Members benefit from some trade diversion in their favour as a result of their membership in an RIA. The rules consequently are limited to preventing the worst forms of discrimination, namely raising barriers against non-RIA members. And since everyone is doing it, of course, nobody really wants the WTO to adopt too tough a line.

The agreements that have the greatest potential to divert trade and merit the closest scrutiny are those between developed countries and high tariff developing countries. The most obvious examples are the free trade agreements between the European Union and North African countries. Given the high external tariffs of these North African countries, it will be difficult for non-EU countries to be competitive in their markets. A similar criticism could be made by the Europeans of the FTAA if it comes to pass.

If everyone is so keen on negotiating more and more bilateral free trade agreements, an obvious question is why not go for a multilateral free trade agreement. Clearly, bilateral free trade agreements are a poor substitute for multilateral free trade. It would be much more efficient to have a single non-discriminatory agreement for everyone rather than a plethora of discriminatory bilateral agreements. But it is easier to negotiate bilateral agreements and everyone thinks that they can gain some advantage over their competitors. The politics works in favour of bilateral agreements, hence their popularity.

One of the big achievements of a successful Millennium Round would be to get tariffs down as close to zero as possible. This would make the RIAs divert less trade and help to improve the efficiency of the global economy. For Canada, it would reduce the benefits of NAFTA, but would create opportunities to diversify trade. That wouldn't be such a bad thing given the current concentration of Canadian trade with the United States.

The Millennium Round could also, perhaps, as part of its institutional review of the WTO, strengthen the provisions of Article XXIV. One possibility would be to be more specific about how long the RIA participants would have to eliminate all tariff barriers among themselves. This would require the participants to go all the way to a customs union or a free trade area and not to enter into a discriminatory trade agreements of indefinite duration.

   Trade blocks themselves, other than the European Union, will not play a big role as participants in the Millennium Round. Only the European Union and South African Customs Union negotiated jointly in the Uruguay Round. Mercosur should negotiate jointly if it is going to become a real customs union, but the trade conflict between Argentina and Brazil after last year's devaluation of the Brazilian *real* make joint participation problematic. Once again, except for the EU, it will again be individual countries around the table.

   There is also the question of the role of the Asia Pacific Economic Co-operation (APEC) in the Millennium Round. APEC, while not a real RIA, includes the United States, Japan, Canada, and eighteen other Pacific economies (the word "countries" is a not used because of the membership of Hong Kong and Taiwan). It's APEC's sheer size, accounting for over half of world output as well as more than half of the world's population, and its potential to introduce discriminatory measures that has worried outsiders, including most notably the Europeans, rather than anything APEC has actually done. So far, except for launching the Information Technology Agreement, which became multilateral, and an aborted effort to achieve sectoral trade liberalization, APEC has limited itself to enunciating grandiose targets for regional free trade by 2010 for developed countries and 2020 for developing countries. In the declaration emanating from the APEC's leaders' meeting in Auckland in September, the leaders passed the ball for trade liberalization to the WTO calling for a comprehensive three-year round of multilateral negotiations. APEC will not be a force in the Millennium Round. So the Europeans can stop worrying.

Chapter 3

Finally Time for Agriculture

THE STAKES ARE HIGH

Negotiators at the Uruguay Round left a couple of land mines embedded in the WTO Agreements for those who would dare to follow in their footsteps. The most explosive of these is the requirement to undertake negotiations on agricultural trade before the year 2000. Not wanting to rush things, WTO Members are waiting to the dying days of the century to comply with this commitment.

In spite of the valiant efforts of scores of trade negotiators over the decades, agriculture has remained largely outside the multilateral trading system. Now the discrepancy between how trade in industrial goods and trade in agriculture is treated in the WTO Agreements has become rather too embarrassing to ignore. It stands as a painful reminder of our negotiating fallibility. What's more, it is something that the developing world will tolerate for only so long. Negotiators at the Millennium Round need to come to grips with domestic farm policies and renew attempts to inflict a stronger rules-based system on agricultural trade.

Agriculture almost scuttled the Uruguay Round and is certain to generate some tense moments in the upcoming set of negotiations. But there is reason to believe that the time might be ripe to make serious progress. Agricultural prices have generally rallied since the Uruguay Round. While governments are still pursuing misguided domestic policies, some of the worst lunacy has been curbed. Although a series of trade disputes means their relationship is far from cozy, at least the US and EU are not deep in the midst of a trade war over agriculture, as they were back in the late 1980s. They might therefore be more disposed to constructive compromise.

Canada has a huge stake in the negotiation of clear rules for agricultural trade. Our abundant land and advantageous climate give us a natural advantage in certain types of production, notably grains, oilseeds and red meat. However, we do not have the financial resources to compete against the treasuries of Europe and the United States. As a result of decades of profligate subsidization, agricultural markets are in disarray. For many commodities, world market prices bear little relation to the cost of production and do not correspond to the price paid in any domestic market. Rather, they are the result of food surpluses dumped by countries that maintain impenetrable import barriers. Until some discipline is imposed on domestic agricultural policies, it is unrealistic to expect farmers to earn their living solely on the basis of world market prices that are both depressed and highly unstable.

THE CONTEXT

Nobody said that this was going to easy. Agriculture policy is exceedingly complex and multi-faceted. It extends to areas quite remote from traditional farming considerations to environmental and regulatory matters, to marketing arrangements, to biotechnology, food security, animal welfare and rural development.

Countries care deeply about their farm sectors. This is true even in developed countries where farmers can account for less than five per cent of the work force. Looking at it rationally, it makes little sense to subsidize and protect our agriculture sectors the way governments do, particularly if foreigners are silly enough to practically give surplus food away on world markets. Taxpayers would not tolerate it if we ran our industrial sectors this way. But farming is different. It can be less a job than a way of life. Commuters on autoroutes like looking out at small, picturesque farms as they speed along. It does not occur to the Japanese business man, golf fanatic that he is, that he would be a lot better off if some of his country's inefficient rice farms were turned into 18-hole paradises. Whatever the rationale – some combination of concerns over food security, respect for rural lifestyle and values, regional development considerations – our feelings about agriculture are very deep-seated and complicated. This is why agricultural trade has been so terribly hard to liberalize.

Farming, among the oldest of the professions, has undergone a remarkable transformation in recent years. Technology has vastly increased yields and changed the nature of production. Technological change has affected all facets of the industry – improvements in seed varieties, pest control, fertilizers, antibiotic and other disease treatments in animals, genetic research, harvesting techniques, food transportation and distribution. While food output has grown sharply, market growth has been slow. The result has been mounting production surpluses and a stubborn reluctance on the part of governments to address the issue.

Progress on the agricultural trade file is complicated by the fact that no one has clean hands. This is certainly true of the developed country Members of the WTO. We all have our sacred cows. In Canada, our dairy sector is highly protected along with poultry and egg producers. The sacred cow in Japan and in Korea is rice farming; in the United States it is the sugar and peanut sectors; and in Europe virtually everything that grows is sacred. This means that none of the Quad Members, those who have taken a leadership role on other areas of trade liberalization, can advocate reform with any credibility.

Consider Canada's position on the agriculture negotiations, for example. We want free trade in the cereals sector but are unwilling to compromise on our support to the supply-managed sectors like dairy and poultry. At best, the message we are giving is mixed.

The stalemate has come at a considerable cost. Agriculture has not shared the huge benefits that have accompanied the expansion in world trade. Canada is a case in point. Our industrial exports have grown astronomically over the past decade while net farm income has been in free fall. Farm income levels in the Prairies are hovering around the 1930s level. Critics of the multilateral trade agreement maintain that this is proof positive that trade agreements do not work. However, anyone familiar with the WTO Agreements could tell them that the farm sector has yet to give liberalized trade an honest chance.

THE URUGUAY ROUND AGREEMENT
ON AGRICULTURE

The GATT amounted to little more than a hill of beans for the agriculture sector. The few rules that did exist were poorly disguised attempts to rationalize the trade distorting agricultural policies of developed countries. GATT provided exemptions for this and exceptions for that with the result that governments had a virtual carte blanche to do whatever they pleased. While the Uruguay Round can hardly be accused of liberalizing world trade in agriculture, it at least attempted to codify agriculture policy measures and impose a framework on the system, reducing support measures modestly in the process. It remains for the Millennium Round to take the structure established in the last round and begin the painful process of trade liberalization.

The WTO Agreement on Agriculture accomplished three basic things. The first is that it called on Members to convert a host of non-tariff barriers such as import quotas, voluntary export restraints, variable import levies and minimum prices into bound tariffs. Some of these tariffs ended up to be shamefully high, but at least they are visible and can be more easily addressed in future sets of negotiations. Some examples are the 300 per cent tariff Canada imposes on butter imports, the 550 per cent imposed on rice imports into Japan, the EU's 215 per cent tariff on frozen beef and the 179 per cent tariff imposed on sweet powdered milk imports to the United States. Members must cut the high ex-quota tariffs by an unweighted average of 36 per cent between 1996 and 2000.

The following chart summarizes the results of "tariffication" for selected developed countries.

CHART 5

EFFECTS OF TARIFFICATION FOR SELECTED OECD COUNTRIES' MFN RATE IN 1996

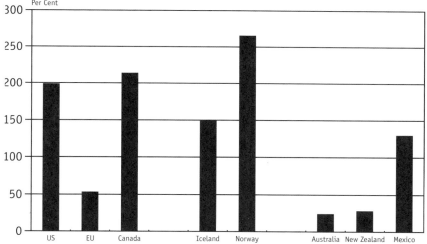

Source: OECD, Indicators of Tariff and Non-tariff Trade Barriers: Update 1997, Table 2.

As part of the "tariffication" exercise, Members also had to provide imports access to a certain percentage of their market. This minimum access commitment applied to 3 per cent of the importer's market, rising to 5 per cent. "Within access" tariffs can be applied by the importing country. In the case of fluid milk imported to Canada, for example, the "within access" tariff rate is 17.5 per cent while the "ex-quota" tariff rate is 284 per cent.

In actual fact, neither the minimum access nor tariff reduction requirements have caused farmers to lose much sleep. The minimum access commitments are very small. A one-third reduction in an astronomical tariff still leaves an astronomical tariff. Various loopholes in the tariff reduction requirements permit countries to cut more deeply in some sectors and reduce others by only 15 per cent in order to meet their overall 36 per cent Uruguay Round obligation. The same pooling of product categories is permitted in order to meet minimum access requirements. There is still plenty of protection left to go around.

The second thing accomplished in the Uruguay Round was to take some tentative steps in the direction of disciplining export subsidies. The Agreement stops well short of prohibiting them altogether, like it does for export subsidies on industrial goods. Instead, Members have agreed not to impose any new farm export subsidies and to cut some existing ones. The Agriculture Agreement lists the type of export subsidies that are subject to the reduction commitments.

Finally, the Uruguay Round tried to make some sense of domestic subsidies. It categorizes domestic support measures into three distinct types – the Green, Blue and Amber Boxes – and subjects some subsidies to reductions according to a schedule of commitments. Certain programs, notably direct payments to producers and income support measures, are not affected by the reduction commitments.

SANITARY AND PHYTO-SANITARY MEASURES

It's easy to spot the authentic trade policy wonks. They are the ones who use the term "sanitary and phyto-sanitary" in cocktail party conversations and even appear to understand what it means.

For those who don't know, sanitary and phyto-sanitary measures are regulations that relate to animal and plant health. Trade policy experts and consumer advocates care deeply about such measures because of their potential to distort world trade. As tariffs and other more conventional types of barriers come down, countries that feel protectionist often resort to technical barriers as a way of restricting imports.

Article 2 of the Agreement on the Application of Sanitary and Phytosanitary Measures asserts the right of Members to establish health and safety standards provided they are based on "sound scientific evidence" and are administered in a consistent manner. Members are also encouraged to rely on international standards whenever possible.

While this is both sensible and fair, administering the Agreement has been quite complicated. Everybody knows that scientists do not always agree. Moreover, countries, like individuals, have vastly different conceptions of what is safe. Imposing one's standards on another, even when accompanied with scientific evidence, is not as easy as it sounds. Consumers confront almost daily stories about things like e-coli, dioxin-contaminated food and mad-cow disease.

Carried away by fear, they pressure their governments to impose higher standards on food safety than might be justified by hard scientific evidence.

All the challenges associated with sanitary and phyto-sanitary standards were played out with vigour in the recent WTO case over beef hormones. The 10-year old EU ban on imports of beef treated with growth enhancing hormones was successfully challenged at the WTO by the United States and Canada. The EU reaction to the case can only be described as one of denial. It has refused to comply with the WTO panel and Appellate Body decision. The WTO, in turn, has permitted the US and Canada to suspend trade privileges on imports from the EU worth US$124 million.

The six hormones at issue are considered safe by the US Food and Drug Administration and by the JECFA, a joint committee of the World Health Organisation and the Food and Agriculture Organisation. However, the EU argues that the hormones are often wrongly implanted and can end up excreting higher than safe levels. It also maintains that accurate tests have yet to be developed to detect some of the most dangerous toxins associated with the hormones. In the meantime, it has sponsored a series of new risk assessment studies and is awaiting the outcome of 17 ongoing studies before deciding how to respond to the panel's decision.

The issue of sanitary and phyto-sanitary measures is one of the thorniest facing negotiators in the upcoming round. The challenge promises to get even more complicated with the promotion of genetically modified organisms by companies like Monsanto. Resistence to food made from genetically modified crops is particularly strong in Europe. Among the events scheduled for Seattle is an antibiotech "teach-in" aimed at trade policy officials.

On one side of the negotiating issue are countries like Canada and the United States that favour a science-based approach. Canada's position is understandable in light of our experience. Canadian exporters have faced a battery of foreign restrictions ranging from bans on canola and beef sales to Europe, salmon and pork exports to Australia and bottled water exports to South Korea. Stronger disciplines in this area would reduce the potential for arbitrary and discriminatory impediments to trade.

The EU position is that WTO rules are inadequate for regulating genetically modified organisms and hormones. It would like to see more recognition of the precautionary principle that would permit restrictions provided the scientific evidence does not rule out the possibility of a risk to safety or health. In Europe's view, current WTO rules place too much onus on the country with the safety concern to justify its trade restriction. In the end, negotiators will have to maneouvre between two quite different perspectives: that consumer concerns should prevail or that scientific evidence should be the determining factor in deciding whether restrictions are warranted.

There are no easy solutions mostly because there is very little common ground. Labeling can paper over some concerns, but only when the importing country concedes that safety is not a real threat. The EU ruled out the labeling option in the hormones case, for example.

The WTO might have to give some credence to the concerns of consumers and non-governmental organizations over food safety. After all, having important WTO Members like the EU refusing to comply with WTO decisions respecting sanitary and phyto-sanitary standards is a blow to the multilateral trading system. At the same time, negotiators must resist pressures to abandon scientific principles entirely. Member governments have to do a better job of promoting the scientific model within their own food regulatory agencies and engendering consumer confidence in it. Countries need to be encouraged to harmonize their standards and rely on international standards as much as possible. This argues for better institutions to conduct basic research in the area, share findings and develop scientific consensus. Another answer might be to create an international scientific body that would operate at an arm's length from governments and provide advice to domestic regulatory agencies and WTO panels.

Issues of biotechnology and food safety impinge heavily on national sovereignty. Pushing too hard and fast in this highly emotional area will only weaken support for trade liberalization generally. The basic axiom should be that more information is better than less. If consumers are properly informed, they will make the right choices. Ultimately, this is in the best interests of food producers and food consumers alike.

MARKET ACCESS

The Uruguay Round made agricultural import barriers far more visible. However, the Agreement called for only cursory reductions in these barriers. It is now up to negotiators in the Millennium Round to begin the difficult process of cutting tariffs and expanding market access.

There are various options for cutting tariffs, ranging from across-the-board cuts, zero-for-zero offers or graduated reductions that would affect higher tariffs more deeply. Chances are that some hybrid approach will be necessary. An overriding objective must be to ensure that the most protected sectors face meaningful reductions. The huge triple-digit tariffs should be addressed with a vengeance. US sugar beet and sugar cane growers, Japanese rice farmers and

Canadian dairy producers should all feel a little less comfortable when the round is over.

As part of the tariff reduction exercise, the special safeguard mechanism will have to be reassessed. Currently, where ex-quota imports increase, a special safeguard can be invoked to block the imports. The trigger thresholds – both price and volume – for initiating the safeguards are easily attained. They should be made stricter in the next round of negotiations.

This means a balanced approach to tariff reduction and market access expansion. It should no longer be possible for countries to shield their most sensitive sectors from foreign competition by pooling their market access commitments into broad categories and selectively improving access within the category.

The market access loophole created in Uruguay Round is illustrated by the example of the sugar imports to the United States. In meeting its Uruguay Round market access commitment, the United States provides raw sugar imports access to some 15 per cent of its market. However, imports of refined sugar, the more value-added product, is restricted to a mere 0.2 per cent of the market. Because the access commitment is for a broad product category, the US maintains that it has complied with its WTO commitment. Fortunately for its sugar refiners, and unfortunately for ours, it has hardly done so in an even-handed fashion.

An obvious solution is to require separate market access commitments for each distinct product. These would be based on the size of the importing country's market for individual products. In Canada's case, this would no longer mean an overall import quota for cheese but separate access for Cheddar, Brie, Emmental and other varieties.

In addition to requiring separate market access commitments for individual products, these commitments should be expanded in the next round. A minimum initial level of 5 per cent of the market and a doubling to 10 per cent over the next five years is a reasonable objective for negotiators. It goes without saying that countries might have to adjust "within quota" tariff rates to ensure that their new minimum access commitments can be met.

EXPORT SUBSIDIES

The Cairns Group has operated as the moral conscience of the agricultural trading world for over a decade. The group represents 15 agricultural exporting nations, including Australia, Brazil, Canada, Chile, and South Africa but conspicuously not the United States or European Union. In its latest meeting of members, the Cairns Group calls for the complete elimination of export subsidies in the next round of negotiations.

It is a bit of a chicken and egg scenario. Countries will be unwilling to abandon export subsidies unless they are sure that world markets will provide farm producers a decent return. However, an improvement in prices and market stability depend on the elimination of the highly distorting export subsidies.

Fortunately, the always interesting internal dynamic of the European Union might give agricultural trade negotiations a boost. The cost to Brussels of providing subsidies to all members in an ever-enlarging European Union is proving increasingly hard to bear. Questions are also being asked about why farmers are entitled to exactly the same levels of financial support, irrespective of whether they live in Portugal, Britain or France. Pressures to "nationalize" Europe's Common Agricultural Policy could give Millennium Round negotiators the opportunity they need to achieve an agreement to phase out export subsidies.

Care will have to be taken to ensure that other types of support are not used as a replacement for export subsidies. Better rules might be necessary, for example, concerning the use of export credit, guarantee and assistance programmes.

SUPPORTING FARMERS IN WAYS THAT DO NOT DISTORT WORLD MARKETS

Elsewhere in the WTO Agreements, the symbol of coloured traffic lights are used to denote subsidy categories. To make things complicated, the Agriculture Agreement uses coloured boxes.

Green Box subsidies have little or no trade-distorting effects. Included in this category are such things as advisory and marketing services and farm support programmes that are "decoupled" from production in that payments are not contingent on production levels. Green box subsidies cannot be challenged by foreign governments and do not have to be reduced.

The Blue Box subsidies category was created in a last-ditch effort to salvage agriculture negotiations during the Uruguay Round. US and EU direct payment programmes fall into the Blue Box category. Somewhat to the consternation of other countries, blue box subsidies do not have to be reduced as part of the overall subsidy reduction commitments.

The final category is the Amber Box. Amber box subsidies can cause distortions to trade and are subject to reduction commitments.

Since the Uruguay Round, WTO Members have made a concerted effort to operate domestic support programmes in a manner consistent with Green Box principles. Programmes have gradually been shifting from price supports and per unit or per acre subsidies towards crop and income insurance plans. The newer breed of subsidy programs are more akin to stabilization schemes and are occasionally tied to the use of responsible environmental practices. The fact that financial assistance is better targeted and is independent of production levels has reduced trade distortions and improved agricultural markets. Even the United States and European Union have implemented farm support packages that appear to be quite compatible with many of the Green Box conditions. While progress has been made, there is still much more to be accomplished.

Millennium Round negotiators should strive to eliminate the Blue Box category, thereby opening the trade distorting domestic support programmes of the US and EU to the possibility of trade challenge and subsidy reduction commitments. The EU is certain to resist this attempt, claiming that its producers are entitled to additional protection because of the higher standards of food and environmental safety they observe. Other countries should not be dissuaded by Europe's argument, however. Even if it were true that Europe's farmers are more concerned with health and environmental matters, they can always be rewarded with decoupled subsidies that do not distort world trade.

As with market access, negotiators will have to be vigilant to ensure that subsidy reductions are accomplished in a balanced fashion. Up until now, countries have been able to comply with the letter of their commitment but ignore the spirit by reducing some subsidies but keeping others high. Reduction commitments need to be made on a disaggregated basis to ensure that all sectors are brought into the multilateral trading system.

MANAGING SUPPLY MANAGEMENT

Supply management is unquestionably the single hardest issue facing Canada's agricultural trade negotiating team. It is certainly the one that will get them into the biggest heat back home. Accustomed as our negotiators are to championing the cause of freer trade, having to switch sides and fight to shield our dairy, chicken and egg sector from foreign competition, all the while keeping a straight face, cannot be an easy task.

In truth, Canada's supply management system is hardly the worst example of agricultural protectionism in action. It does result in higher consumer costs but Canada's food prices are amongst the lowest in the world and significantly lower than those in Europe. Proponents of supply management maintain that it results in stable and predictable markets that benefit both producers and consumers. What's more, it accomplishes this without bleeding the government treasury dry. Unlike the US sugar or European grain programmes, Canada's supply management system controls production and generates only minimal food surpluses. Hence, it is not nearly as trade distorting as other types of agricultural support.

The difficulty with Canada's supply management system is that it has to severely restrict imports in order to work. Otherwise, lower import prices would undermine the much higher domestic support prices. The second problem with supply management is that it is rather insidious. To maintain high domestic price levels, a host of substitute products, processed products and generally related products have to be regulated too. For example, margarine has to be on the import control list or the high domestic butter prices would seem out of wack. The list of dairy blends that are subject to import restrictions grows by the day, along with the ingenuity of American processors for developing new recipes using powdered milk. Frozen pizza makers, chicken-pot-pie producers and other food manufacturers dependent on supply managed products all have to be taken care of to ensure that they stay competitive with foreign producers who use much cheaper food inputs.

An example of the kind of trouble we have created for ourselves is illustrated by the American and New Zealand WTO challenge to Canada's milk pricing system. The Canadian system works by guaranteeing milk producers a high price for milk they sell to the domestic market, provided they do not produce more than their production quota. Farmers can produce more than the quota amount and sell it on world markets but only at the considerably lower world price. Canadian food processors are allowed to buy industrial milk at the lower world market price for production that they are intending to export. The rationale is that they would not be able to compete against foreign processors if they had to pay the high domestic prices for their milk requirements.

In the opinion of the WTO panel, Canada's two-tiered pricing system amounts to an export subsidy to dairy processors. A recent WTO Appellate Body ruling upheld the panel's view. While it should be fairly easy to change the milk pricing system to comply with this particular WTO ruling, it should give us reason to reflect on the future of supply management.

There are good made-in-Canada arguments for reforming the supply management system. It rigidly controls production and restricts internal trade with the result that farms are probably smaller and less efficient than they would otherwise be. The more stringent the restrictions are, the more valuable the production quota becomes to those who hold it. Quota-holders have a huge stake in perpetuating the status quo and are willing to fight hard to protect it. To make matters even worse, there is a Canadian unity angle. A disproportionate number of Canada's dairy producers live in Quebec. All in all, it is little wonder that governments have been reluctant to take the issue on.

While our supply management system survived the Uruguay Round pretty well intact, it might not be so lucky in the next set of negotiations. There will be pressure to expand market access commitments which, combined with trade challenges to the two-tiered pricing system, could spell the beginning of the end for high domestic support prices.

To date, Canada's response has been to stick its head in the sand. Our government does not want to be even seen to be advancing a position or it would be eaten alive by the supply-management boards and producers. This is unfortunate for a couple of reasons. First, it means we are not able to play a meaningful role in other areas of the agricultural trade agenda where Canada could gain much from better trade disciplines. Second, we also risk being left out in the cold in last-minute deals affecting supply management. We are marginal players in the agriculture trade scene. The real action occurs in the US-EU arena and, to some extent, in the Cairns Group where Australia is particularly active. Our only hope for influencing the outcome to our advantage is to be active and constructive participants from the very outset.

STATE TRADING

Fingers are almost certain to be pointed Canada's way in the next round of trade negotiations over state trading enterprises. State trading enterprises are government-sponsored monopolies engaged in the export or import business. One of the most notorious is the Canadian Wheat Board.

The Canadian Wheat Board has long operated as the sole exporter of Canadian grain. Its scale of operation is thought to give it an advantage in foreign markets over private sellers who deal in smaller quantities. The United States has launched a series of trade challenges at the Wheat Board on the grounds that it secretly subsidizes exports. So far, none of the US challenges have found their mark but it might yet get its way in the Millennium Round.

Given the havoc big export-subsidizers like the United States have inflicted over the years on international grain markets, picking on the Canadian Wheat Board is a bit like the pot calling the kettle black. Sadly for the Board, however, it has some detractors in its own back yard. Many Canadian grain producers are also frustrated at the Board's monopoly power since it prevents them from marketing their grain directly or with private companies.

It is quite likely that negotiators will agree that state trading enterprises should be more transparent. For example, these entities could be required to disclose more details about their revenues and financial dealings. More complete information about their operations would placate the concerns of domestic constituents as well.

Attention in the next negotiating round will also focus on state-sponsored import monopolies like the Canadian Dairy Commission and provincial liquor boards. The concern there is that such bodies act to unfairly restrict imports. Many of the newly acceding WTO Members, notably those from former centrally-planned economies, rely heavily on state trading enterprises to handle importation. Over time, the problem should become less urgent as expansions in minimum access requirements loosen their monopoly over imports. In the meantime, they should also have to become more transparent operations.

GOING BANANAS

The relative absence of rules governing agricultural trade has meant that food fights have figured very prominently in the work of the WTO dispute settlement body. One of the most notorious battles has been over bananas. Not only has the bananas case severely tested the mettle of the WTO's Dispute Settlement Undertaking but it has raised some very complicated questions about preferential trading agreements, development assistance and the compliance provisions of the WTO dispute settlement regime.

The United States, spurred on by three home-grown banana heavy-weights, Dole, Chiquita and Del Monte, successfully challenged the European Union's preferential marketing practices for bananas. The European system is a tangled collection of tariffs and quotas aimed at supporting producers in former colonies in the Africa, Carribean, and Pacific Region (ACP countries). Europe feels duty-bound to protect growers in their former colonies by granting them exclusive access to its market. The United States views bananas as big business and well as strategic politics.

Despite having lost the case, the EU has refused to implement the WTO ruling and bring its practices immediately into compliance. Disagreements within the EU over how to proceed are delaying action. Old colonial powers like France don't want to do anything that will weaken their ties with their banana-producing, former colonies. Countries like Germany that have not had colonies in recent years are more interested in cheaper bananas and avoiding US trade sanctions. In the meantime, while the EU dillydallies, the WTO has granted the United States permission to impose close to $200 million worth of retaliatory tariffs against European imports as compensation.

Cartoon by Jeff Danziger, *Los Angeles Times* Syndicate, April 15, 1999. Reprinted with permission of Jeff Danziger.

The European quotas make for bad trade policy and bad development policy. The system results in prices in Europe that are roughly twice US levels. However, little of this extra consumer spending finds its way to banana growers in recipient nations as most is hived away by European importers and wholesalers. Arguably, this money could be much better devoted to direct cash assistance to banana-producing countries. Within the developing nations, the production quotas separate growers into haves and have-nots. Those lucky enough to hold export licenses are substantially better off than their unendowed brethren. As with Canada's system of production and import quotas for supply managed commodities, the banana quotas have fostered a convoluted regime of rent-seeking.

In the end, Europe's former colonies would be far better off with a better WTO deal on agriculture. This is where the EU's precious energy should be devoted.

AN AGENDA FOR ACTION

The Millennium Round will be judged a failure unless meaningful progress is made liberalizing trade in food and food products. It's high time that agriculture gets dragged kicking and screaming into the multilateral trading system.

The onus is on the developed world to make this happen and to demonstrate to developing country members that the WTO is an institution that serves their objectives too.

Success will depend on achieving progress in all the critical negotiating areas of market access, reform of domestic support measures, export subsidies and sanitary and phyto-sanitary barriers. Though quite different ways of protecting the farm sector, they are highly interrelated. The danger is that as one area gets subjected to greater trade disciplines, governments could well search out other trade-distorting ways to shore up producers.

It is not too late for Canada to begin to show some leadership on agriculture. We can only talk out of two sides of our mouth for so long. Canadian farmers have a natural advantage in the production of some commodities like oilseeds, grains and red meat. Yet, our ability to participate in world markets is hamstrung by our refusal to engage in discussions over supply management. We should be willing to undertake constructive reforms to our supply management system in exchange for changes to the considerably more egregious farm programmes of our major trading partners. Unless we are willing to go down this path, we take the chance that a solution will be foisted on us in the Millennium Round. That is hardly in the best interest of Canadian farmers.

Chapter 4

Second Crack at Services

TRADE IN SERVICES BOOMING

Although trade in services is only a fraction of trade in goods (one fifth for Canada), it has been growing much more rapidly. Between 1990 and 1997, exports of commercial services grew 8 per cent per year while merchandise exports only increased 6 ½ per cent. By 1997, exports of commercial services had surpassed US$1.3 trillion, and accounted for almost one fifth of total exports. And there is still plenty of room for growth. Services are the mainstay of modern industrialized economies, accounting for almost two-thirds of output and more than two-thirds of employment.

Trade in services is important for the three main areas of the world. North America's share of world exports of services is almost 20 per cent; Europe's almost 46 per cent; and Asia's almost 23 per cent.

The most dynamic component of services trade is not the traditional transportation or travel services, but other services which include fast-growing financial services, construction services, and computer and information services. Services are at the heart of the new information economy. It is these services that are key in raising productivity in the production of goods and in making an economy more competitive.

Services are not like goods, which cross borders in neatly-stacked boxes that can be inspected by customs officers and subjected to duties and other tax-like measures. Their flow is invisible. The barriers to trade in services are usually regulatory inside the border rather than border measures like tariffs and quotas. A trading regime for services has to be different from one for goods.

THE GATS

By the time the Uruguay Round got underway in 1986, trade in services, like the camel in the tent, had become too important to be ignored any longer. Notwithstanding strong resistance at the outset from many developing countries, the General Agreement on Trade in Services, which was negotiated over this round, represents a first effort to establish multilateral, legally-enforceable rules for trade in services. Patterned on the GATT, it covers all services, except those provided in the exercise of governmental authority, and seeks to ensure transparency in regulations and inquiry points. It also specifies that regulations must be "administered in a reasonable, objective and impartial manner," and that international payments with respect to covered trade in services should normally be unrestricted.

Most fundamentally, the GATS seeks to implement the two key basic principles of non-discrimination – most-favoured-nation and national treatment, which are the core of the GATT. Unfortunately though, as for many copies, the original was much better. In the GATS, the MFN principle allows exceptions and national treatment applies only in certain sectors and subject to such limitations as specified in each WTO Member's schedule of commitments.

The GATS covers all four ways or "modes" of providing an international service:

- *cross-border supply* of services sold from a supplier in one country to customers in another (e.g. overseas telephone calls);
- *consumption abroad* of services in another country by nationals of a different country (e.g. hotels and tourism);
- *commercial presence* of subsidiaries or branches in another country to supply services (e.g. foreign insurance company branches);
- *presence of natural persons* in another country to supply a service (e.g. accountants).

Because the GATS imposes obligations with respect to the "commercial presence" of foreign service suppliers in a country, it effectively covers investment abroad. This makes it the first multilateral investment agreement. And it was negotiated without all the muss and fuss of the MAI.

The MFN principle as applied to the GATS means that, if a country allows foreign services or service suppliers market access, it must allow equal access for all services and service suppliers of the other Members of the WTO. The qualification is that countries are permitted to list exceptions to MFN treatment in individual sectors. These exceptions could only be made at the time of the initial agreement, and no more can be added. By April 15, 1994 when the Final Act of the Uruguay Round was signed, 61 lists of such exceptions had been submitted. The exceptions are to be reviewed after five years and are to end after ten years. Countries are expected to remove the exceptions even sooner when other countries agree to reciprocal market access commitments such as has already occurred in basic telecommunications and financial services. The principle of MFN treatment should eventually become unqualified as it already is for the GATT (except of course for customs unions and free trade areas which are allowed under both agreements).

The GATS also imposes a national treatment obligation. This means that foreign and national services and service suppliers must be given equal treatment under the regulations governing applicable service sectors. But there is a very big qualifier attached. The national treatment obligation only applies when a country makes a positive commitment in its schedule. In contrast, the national treatment obligation in the GATT applies generally. Once a good is admitted across the border, it can not be subjected to discriminatory taxes, regulations or other internal measures. If this was too ambitious for the countries negotiating, it would have been better, at a minimum, to have incorporated a national treatment obligation in the GATS that was subject to specific listed exceptions in a schedule (the so-called negative list). Such an approach would have been more transparent and the nature of the benefits accruing from the obligation more ascertainable.

The situation is not quite as bad as it seems with respect to national treatment, however. Once a country makes a commitment with respect to a sector, national treatment applies to all services in the given sector unless the country enters a reservation. Hence another problem: these reservations tend to be very broad. An effort needs to be made to make the reservations as narrow as possible.

The schedules of commitments with respect to national treatment under the GATS serve the same role as the tariff schedules under the GATT. They are the focus of the negotiations to improve market access. A country will offer to accord national treatment in a specific sector in return for national treatment in the same or different sector from another country. These concessions are in turn "multilateralized" so that all parties to the negotiation can enjoy the benefit. Specific commitments are binding in the same way as tariff commitments are binding under the GATT. They provide a reasonable assurance of stability in market access and can only be withdrawn with compensation.

There are twelve broad sectors listed in the GATS schedules of commitments, which follows the GATT Secretariat's classification scheme. Within this broad framework, commitments are specified by numerical references to the Central Product Classification System of the United Nations. By July of this year, there were 132 schedules of specific commitments submitted and agreed. Their sectoral distribution is shown in Table 1. The sector with by far the most commitments was tourism and travel related services. Even the least developed countries are keen on attracting foreign investment in tourism and travel. Financial services, business services and communication services also have relatively large number of commitments. In financial services and communication services, the number of commitments went up as a result of the Financial Services and the Basic Telecommunications Agreements reached after the conclusion of the Uruguay Round.

Table 1
Specific Commitments by Sector

01. Business Services	89
02. Communication Services	85
03. Construction and Related Engineering Services	60
04. Distribution Services	38
05. Educational Services	32
06. Environmental Services	40
07. Financial Services	91
08. Health Related and Social Services	34
09. Tourism and Travel Related Services	114
10. Recreational, Cultural and Sporting Services	49
11. Transport Services	70
12. Other Services not Included Elsewhere	9
Total	711

Source: http:www.wto.org/wto/services/websum.htm
       dated 7/31/1999.

The industrialized countries with their more developed service sectors have been the ones most willing to make commitments for more sectors. Developing countries, particularly the least developed, have been the least willing. The European Union has made commitments with respect to all twelve sectors. The United States and Japan have made commitments with respect to eleven sectors including all sectors but the residual "other" category. Canada has only made commitments for eight sectors, leaving out educational services, health related and social services, and recreational, cultural and sporting services as well as the "other" category. This reflects Canada's traditional concerns about education and health, which is largely in the public sector, and worries about external, especially American, threats to Canadian culture.

The GATS allows governments to negotiate agreements to recognize qualifications for the purpose of authorizing, licensing or certifying service providers. But in order to prevent these mutual recognition agreements from being discriminatory and becoming additional barriers to trade, it requires that all WTO Members be given an adequate opportunity to join them. WTO Members are also required to work together to establish common international standards and criteria for the recognition and practice of the trades and professions involved in the international delivery of services.

The GATS is overseen by the Council for Trade in Services. This body, made up of representatives of all the member countries, serves the same function for the GATS as the Council for Trade in Goods serves for the GATT. Members must notify the Council for Trade in Services of any changes in regulations affecting services covered by specific commitments and of any recognition agreements for qualifications. Domestic regulations are the main form of barriers for service trade. That is why a Working Group on Regulation has been established.

Trade in services has aspects that make it unique. And some types of services are quite different from others. This is reflected in some of the GATS annexes:

- *Movement of Natural Persons* This annex establishes the right of an individual providing a service to temporarily stay in a country and makes the distinction between such an individual and any individual seeking employment or to immigrate.
- *Air Transport Services* This annex limits the coverage of the GATS to the relatively minor categories of aircraft repair and maintenance, the marketing of air transport services, and computer reservation services. The more important traffic rights are excluded to remain under the current system of bilateral air service agreements, whereby a country grants another country's carriers landing rights in exchange for landing rights in the other country.
- *Financial Services* This annex, which defines financial services, excludes the activities of central banks, and social security or public retirement funds from coverage and makes clear the governments' right to take prudential measures to protect the public and to ensure the integrity and stability of the financial system.
- *Telecommunication Services* This annex requires governments to provide foreign service providers access to public telecommunications networks

and services on a reasonable and non-discriminatory basis. This is important because some service suppliers absolutely need access to supply their services. For example, money transfers, on-line information services and data-base retrieval require good communication links to operate. Providing access to the network is not the same thing as opening up the market to supply public telecommunication services. That would require a further specific commitment.

SUBSEQUENT NEGOTIATIONS

The Uruguay Round was not the end of service sector negotiations, but rather the beginning. Negotiations continued in four areas: basic telecommunication services; financial services; movement of natural persons; and maritime transport. Agreements were reached on basic telecommunication services and financial services by early 1997. Concerning movement of natural persons, guidelines and disciplines have been developed for the accountancy sector as a model for facilitating trade in professional services. More general talks to improve specific commitments in the movement of natural persons were completed in July 1995 without any concrete results. Negotiations on maritime transport, which had earlier proved difficult in the context of both the Canada-US Free Trade Agreement and GATT, were suspended in 1996.

TELECOMMUNICATION SERVICES

No commitments were made during the Uruguay Round on basic telecommunications services. The fact that basic telecommunication services were delivered by government monopolies in many countries, including those in Europe at the time of the completion of the round in 1994, made the liberalization of trade in this sector a tricky business. It was much easier to liberalize trade in some of the more value-added telecommunication services. Some commitments covering these services such as allowing third-party supply of Private Branch Exchanges found their way into some of the original GATS schedules. But the big prize – the $675 billion market for basic telecommunication services including local, long distance and international services for home and business – was left for further negotiations.

A path-breaking agreement was finally reached on February 15, 1997 liberalizing trade in basic telecommunication services. By the time the agreement came into force on February 5, 1998, 72 countries representing over 90 per cent of the market had submitted commitments on basic telecommunication services, including 59 countries that committed to a complete set of "reference rules" for regulating the telecommunications sector. These rules require countries to open their market to foreign investment and competition, to establish an independent telecommunications regulator, to make interconnection guarantees, and to agree to WTO surveillance. Commitments made by most governments covered local, long-distance and international voice services, data transmission, cellular/mobile markets, leased circuits, and satellite services. Some of the commitments are subject to a phase-in period.

As a general rule, the benefits of the Telecommunications Agreement are extended to all WTO Members on a MFN basis. But each signatory was given the option of filing an MFN exemption, which 9 countries actually submitted. This included an American exemption for one-way satellite transmission of Direct-to-Home (DTH) and Direct Broadcast Satellite (DBS) television services and digital audio services.

The liberalization of the market for telecommunication services before the agreement entered into force had already lead to dramatically lower phone rates in North America and Britain. In 1998, the Europeans were already moving to privatize state monopoly telecommunication companies and to liberalize the market for telecommunication services. The WTO Telecommunications Agreement will help them to secure the benefits of lower telephone rates and improved quality of services. The over 46 participating developing and transition economies with telecommunication rates that are 10 or 20 times those in North America will also benefit.

While Canada refused to allow majority foreign ownership of telecommunication companies, there were major changes here as well. Teleglobe Inc., which lost its monopoly on overseas calls for Canadian carriers, has managed to sell services to carriers world-wide. The Telesat monopoly on fixed satellites is scheduled to end in March 2000.

FINANCIAL SERVICES

Even though many countries made specific commitments on market access and national treatment during the Uruguay Round, the offers were not considered sufficient to call an end to the negotiations by the time of the Marrakesh Ministerial Meeting in April 1994. Treatment was still based on reciprocity and broad exemptions to the MFN principle persisted. The negotiations in the financial sector were extended until June 1995, six months after the coming into force of the GATS. These negotiations, which resulted in a modest "interim agreement," also proved not to be enough. Again negotiations were resumed. Fortunately, these proved to be more fruitful.

The Asian financial crisis touched off by the devaluation of the Thai baht in July 1997 held the feet of some previously recalcitrant negotiators to the fire. This facilitated the negotiation of a new and improved set of financial services commitments under the GATS. The process culminated on December 12, 1997, when 71 countries agreed to the new Financial Services Agreement. This gave an important signal to the world that the Asian crisis was not going to be allowed to derail the move to more open global financial markets.

The new pact, which brought to 104 the number of countries with commitments in financial services, came into force on March 1, 1999. It covers more than 90 per cent of the enormous global market for financial services, which takes in $40 trillion in domestic bank lending, $20 trillion in securities trading, and over $2 trillion in insurance premiums.

The Financial Services Agreement lightens or scraps regulatory restrictions on foreign banks, securities firms, and insurance companies. The new commitments made included the elimination or relaxation of restrictions on foreign ownership, the juridical form of commercial presence, and the expansion of existing operations. WTO Members have also undertaken to do something about measures that enforce the segmentation of banking, securities and insurance or that restrict geographical expansion. This is important in the United States where the Glass-Steagall Act and the McFadden Acts restrict opportunities for foreign financial institutions.

In the final agreement, the United States, India and Thailand withdrew their broad reciprocity-based MFN exemptions. Several other countries also curtailed the scope of their exemptions. The United States submitted a new MFN exemption in insurance, which was targeted at Malaysia but was made generally applicable to countries that force US insurance companies to divest.

Canada's new financial service commitment reaffirmed the Government's previously announced intention to permit foreign banks to directly open branches in Canada. It also allowed foreign bank subsidiaries operating in Canada to open branches. This was something that US and Mexican banks already could do under the NAFTA.

The United States, which was the driving force behind the financial service talks, expects to be the big winner as the agreement opens up global markets to the highly competitive US financial services industry. In spite of what four of Canada's six biggest banks said about the need to be bigger to survive when they were trying to justify mergers, Canada does have world class financial sector and can be a winner too. Moreover, in the end, everyone will gain from freer trade in financial services because of the increased access to lower cost capital ushered in by the agreement.

Even though the financial services agreement marks a big step forward in opening up trade in financial services, many barriers remain. Countries with a comparative advantage in financial services like the United States and the United Kingdom can be expected to push for further liberalization in the Millennium Round.

PROFESSIONAL SERVICES

As a first step towards imposing more disciplines on service sectors involving the professions, the accounting sector was picked as a pilot to develop rules to facilitate trade in these services. First, the WTO Council on Trade in Services adopted guidelines for the recognition of qualifications in the accountancy sector on May 29, 1997. These guidelines, which are non-binding, were prepared to make it easier for governments to conclude agreements on the mutual recognition of professional qualifications. Second, the WTO Council for Trade in Services adopted *Disciplines on Domestic Regulation in the Accounting Sector* on December 14, 1998. These disciplines, which apply to all countries with specific commitments for the accounting sector, cover the administration of licensing requirements, qualification requirements and procedures, technical standards, and transparency requirements. Under the disciplines, regulatory measures can't be more trade-restrictive than necessary to attain such legitimate objectives as protecting consumers, and ensuring the quality of the service and professional competence. These disciplines are to be integrated into the GATS and become legally binding at the end of the next round of service negotiations. In the meantime, WTO Members agreed not to take any inconsistent measures. The work program for accountancy now needs to be extended to other professional services such as engineers, architects and legal consultants.

MARITIME TRANSPORT

Although there are some commitments in the GATS schedules with respect to ocean transport, port facilities and auxiliary services, maritime transport has proved a hard nut to crack for trade negotiators. Countries have many restrictions on maritime transport such as the Jones Act in the United States which limits foreign participation in domestic transport. Failing to reach any agreement during the Uruguay Round, an additional round of marine transport negotiations was scheduled to end in June 1996. All that the group could agree on by that deadline was to suspend the negotiations until the commencement of the next comprehensive service sector negotiations in the year 2000. The

MFN obligations were also suspended, but at least a standstill was imposed on any new barriers. Maritime transport remains a sector where trade barriers abound. Liberalization in maritime transport should be an important objective of the Millennium Round.

THE SERVICE AGENDA

The GATS (Article XIX:1) requires negotiations to begin by the year 2000 to increase the number and level of commitments in countries' schedules. This is a major part of the WTO's built-in agenda that has set the stage for the Millennium Round. Because many more barriers to trade exist in the service sector than in the goods sector and because they take the much more intractable form of regulatory obstacles, further liberalization of trade in services must be a key objective of the Millennium Round. The Uruguay Round was just a beginning. Much must be done before trade in services is as free as trade in goods.

An indication of the magnitude of the task needed to liberalize trade in services is provided by Table 1. The shortfall of the number of specific commitments from the number 134 (the total number of WTO Members when the table was prepared) reveals the number of WTO Members that have not made commitments to liberalize in a specific sector. For instance, the existence of just 91 commitments in financial services means that 43 WTO Members have not made commitments. Only 70 Members have signed the Financial Services Agreement, leaving 64 that have not. The cup may be either half empty or half full depending on your point of view. But one thing is clear; it's not full. In addition, only 38 WTO Members have made commitments in distribution services, leaving 96 that have not. This is important because an open distribution system with equal access is important for providing access to goods. If your goods aren't on the shelves, they don't get sold. This has been a perennial problem in penetrating the Japanese market. It was the main complaint made by the United States before the WTO in the recent Fuji-Kodak challenge. In this 1997 case, the US argued unsuccessfully that Japanese government measures kept Kodak out of distribution and retailing in Japan.

In subsectors within the sectors, the number of WTO Members that have not made commitments is even higher because a commitment in any subsector counts as a sectoral commitment even if there are no commitments for other subsectors. For example, only 14 WTO Members have made commitments in the audio-visual subsector of the communication sector. This is a particular sore point for the Americans who push US pop culture exports of action movies and rock music.

The differences between goods and services is becoming increasingly blurred. Manufacturing firms are providing financing and ongoing service support to sophisticated high-tech products and service firms are packaging technologically advanced products with their services. Products can no longer be put in hermetically-sealed boxes to be governed by the GATS or the GATT.

Since the GATS is a separate agreement from the GATT, there is an issue of how to handle overlapping topics. For instance, does it make sense to have different rules for investment in service-producing industries than in goods-producing industries as currently exists? What about rules for movement of natural persons? These questions are even more complex for firms that produce goods as well as services. At a minimum, the two agreements have to be consistent and the negotiations coordinated. An alternative would be to carve out the negotiations on the cross-cutting issues and place the disciplines concerning the treatment of enterprises under a separate agreement that would apply regardless of whether the enterprise produced services or goods.

Speaking before the World Services Congress in Washington last June, US Trade Representative Charlene Barshefsky proposed that the "request-offer" approach of the GATS be replaced by a better negotiating approach. She suggested that the "zero-for-zero" and formula approaches, which were used to negotiate tariffs for goods, could be applied to services. Under these approaches, negotiators could agree to get rid of all barriers in a sector or to reduce them to a certain negotiated level. Such a more aggressive approach appears to be more promising than the slow and painstaking process of waiting for countries to offer up the barriers themselves.

Another approach that appears promising is that pursued in the telecommunication negotiations. It involves developing a common regulatory framework for a sector, which would be accepted by all WTO Members. This approach could be systematically applied sector by sector starting with the sectors such as maritime transport where the barriers are the greatest

Rules governing three areas of the GATS were left unfinished in the Uruguay Round: subsidies, safeguards, and government procurement. This was partly because time ran out and partly because it wasn't clear what, if anything, needed to be done. But commitments for future action were made. GATS Article XV requires Members to enter into negotiations to develop disciplines for subsidies. GATS Article XIII promises further multilateral negotiations on government procurement in services.

Subsidies is probably the easiest area to deal with in theory. The same kinds of disciplines that apply to subsidies on goods could be extended to subsidies for services. Disputes over service subsidies could be handled under the dispute settlement system. While export subsidies are not a big problem for services, domestic subsidies in such areas as transportation and telecommunications are very high. They are also extremely difficult to measure. The big problem would be convincing countries that currently make heavy use of subsidies to accept the disciplines. Special rules would have to be negotiated for certain sensitive sectors such as health, education, and pensions where subsidies are used to pursue important social policy objectives.

In the context of trade in goods, safeguards are measures that protect domestic industries from surges in imports. In the past, they were useful in convincing governments to agree to trade liberalization in sensitive areas like agriculture. On the bright side, traded services can't be stored and are thus less subject to surges than imports of goods. Safeguards are consequently less necessary for service imports. Nonetheless, some Members may seek some form of safeguard protection as a trade-off for more liberalized trade in services.

Given that government procurement of goods is not covered by the GATT, it should not be surprising that government procurement of services is not covered by the GATS. Procurement of services is more difficult to deal with than procurement of goods. Procurement of services is characterized by small contracts and difficult issues of determining quality. Nevertheless, there are services such as financial services, transportation, telecommunications, and construction that should be subject to disciplines. The most sensible approach would probably be to convince all WTO Members to become signatories to the plurilateral Government Procurement Agreement rather than establish a separate set of disciplines under GATS. Irrespective of what is done about procurement, there is still the issue of the definition of the government sector excluded under the GATS to be resolved. From the point of view or exerting discipline on as large a share of government procurement as possible, the narrower the definition the better. If the definition were limited to core government or public administration, the GATS obligations would be binding on many government agencies and enterprises and thus would exercise a greater discipline on government procurement of services.

The United States, with its dynamic service sector, is the champion of freer trade in services. Canada's service sector is not that far behind, especially in commercial services, and definitely can use the competition to catch up. A dynamic and competitive service sector is essential for an economy's overall competitiveness. That's another reason why the GATS negotiation is so critical for the success of the Millennium Round.

Chapter 5

Taming Procurement

THE RULES OR LACK THEREOF

Governments like to think that they are a rule unto themselves. Consequently, government procurement has never been subject to the discipline of multilateral trading rules under the WTO and its predecessor GATT. Under Article III:8 of the original GATT 1947, it was excluded from the national treatment obligation for goods. More recently, in the GATS, it was carved out of the main commitments for services. Since procurement of goods and services by governments and their agencies accounts for 10 to 15 per cent of GDP, its non-coverage is an important gap in the international trade covered by multilateral rules. The lack of rules is made even more serious by the fact that government procurement is often not guided by the principle of "best value for money" as determined by fair and open competition on the free market. Instead, it often results from political decisions made behind closed doors. In most countries, purchasing is frequently used to support local firms and regions. This can be the result of specific prohibitions on foreign suppliers, or various types of preferences. Alternatively, it can result from more insidious measures and practices that deny foreign firms the opportunity to bid on government requirements. These include excessive sole source tendering, tailored technical requirements, and a general lack of transparency.

The first successful international effort to tackle the problem of government procurement was made during the Tokyo Round of multilateral trade negotiations. In the first Agreement on Government Procurement that entered into force on January 1, 1981, a select group of participating countries offered to open up their procurement opportunities to other countries in return for access to their procurement markets. This agreement was plurilateral rather than multilateral meaning that, unlike most of other GATT agreements, it applied only to countries that specifically signed on to the Agreement.

The WTO Agreement on Government Procurement, which came into effect on January 1, 1996, is based on the earlier agreements, but expands the scope of coverage to include some services and construction as well as goods by specified public entitities. Purchases of goods and services over SDR 130,000 (over Can $250,000) by governments and agencies are covered and purchases of construction services over SDR 5 million (or around Can $10 million).

The GPA provides an opportunity to bid on more than US$250 billion per year in government contracts. The total value of contracts won by foreign supplies covered by the agreement was US$30 billion based on information collected for the 1990-94 period. The juxtaposition of the large opportunities with the modest results shows that, even with the GPA, foreign suppliers are only getting a small share of the government procurement market.

There are now 26 GPA Member countries, including Canada, the United States, the European Union and Japan, 15 observer governments, and two observer international organizations.

The foundation, on which the Agreement on Government Procurement rests, is the simple, but powerful, principle of non-discrimination or national treatment, which means that member countries are required to give the goods, services, and suppliers of other members treatment that is "no less favorable" than they give their own. To ensure that there is no discrimination, the agreement sets out procedures for providing transparency of laws, regulations, procedures and practices governing procurement. It also establishes norms in respect of technical specifications and tendering procedures and prohibits offsets. Finally, it requires member countries to establish formal bid challenge procedures.

The GPA is not the only procurement agreement to which Canada is a party. The rules governing procurement between Canada and the United States are also covered by Chapter 10 of the NAFTA. And government procurement relations between Canada and Mexico are subject to Chapter 10 of NAFTA, but not the GPA.

Signatory Member Countries of Agreement on Government Procurement			
Austria	Germany	Korea	Singapore
Belgium	Greece	Liechtenstein	Spain
Canada	Hong Kong	Luxembourg	Sweden
Denmark	Ireland	Netherlands	Switzerland
EU	Israel	Netherlands for Aruba	United Kingdom
Finland	Italy	Norway	United States
France	Japan	Portugal	
Observer Governments			
Argentina	Chinese Tapei*	Latvia	Poland
Australia	Columbia	Lithuania	Slovenia
Bulgaria	Estonia	Mongolia	Turkey
Chile	Iceland*	Panama*	
* Negotiating Accession			
Observers – International Organizations			
IMF	OECD		

LIMITATIONS OF THE AGREEMENT

There are important limitations to the scope and coverage of the Agreement on Government Procurement. As a plurilateral agreement, it applies only to member countries and then only to procurement by specified government departments and enterprises, and non-central levels of government. Moreover, its coverage is limited to specified goods, services and construction services, above certain monetary thresholds. The rule is: if it's not specified, it's not covered.

The first limitation is that membership in the Agreement has so far embraced only the major industrialized countries. No developing countries have yet joined, although some are observers. Developing countries generally have the most discriminatory procurement practices, either out of misguided efforts to promote economic development or out of simple corruption. Consequently, they are the members that need to be brought under the Agreement the most, both for their own sakes as well as for the sakes of other members. Their taxpayers would benefit from lower cost goods and services, and other countries would benefit from expanded markets. The United States is pushing to extend the GPA to all WTO Members.

The second important limitation is peculiar to Canada. It's Canada's lack of access to the procurement of non-central levels of government under the Agreement. Since the Canadian Government was not prepared to make commitments with respect to Canada's provincial and local government procurement, other countries are allowed to have derogations from most-favoured-nation status for Canada with respect to their own sub-central government procurement. Canadian exporters are thus not able to benefit fully from the Agreement in obtaining access to procurement by non-central levels of government in other member countries.

Motivated in part by worries about opening up procurement in the health and education sector to foreign suppliers, the Canadian provinces have refused to go along with any deals negotiated by the Canadian Federal Government that would allow the United States to retain Buy American and small business carve-outs. While the concerns about the impact of the GPA in their areas of jurisdiction are legitimate, provinces are going beyond their jurisdiction when they try to dictate to the Canadian federal government on the exact nature of the access deal that must be negotiated with the United States.

It is particularly ironic that Canada, which has a preferential trading relationship with the United States under the NAFTA, has less favorable access to state and local government procurement in the United States than other countries such as the European Union and Japan, which have no such special trading arrangement. Canadian suppliers have their provincial governments to thank for this.

The third important limitation pertains to the scope and coverage of the Agreement that is set out in the general notes provided in the appendix of each signatory. Important listed exclusions include urban transportation and defence, and set asides for small and minority businesses.

There are also technical problems with the Agreement. Many of the procedures specified are unnecessarily complex and need to be updated to reflect the way business is currently being done using computers and modern telecommunications. For instance, the forty-day period for tendering is considered unduly long now with computerized bidding for many goods and services, and the requirements that invitations to participate in an intended procurement be published in a listed publication and that "tenders normally be submitted in writing either directly or by mail" are not consistent with computerized procurement systems. Accepted modes of transmission of information in the

Agreement need to be brought into the information age and should include e-mail.

A review of the Agreement on Government Procurement as required under Article XXIV:7 is currently underway in the WTO Committee on Government Procurement, which is made up of representatives of signatories of the Agreement, and is scheduled to be ready this fall. The review is aimed at simplifying the administrative rules in the Agreement and making them consistent with current business practice. It is also seeking to cover more procurement and to eliminate "discriminatory measures" or exceptions to coverage. An effort is being made to complete these negotiations before the Seattle Ministerial. These improvements are expected to increase the attractiveness of the GPA to other prospective new members.

The Canadian Government, under pressure from the provinces, has been preoccupied with bilateral Canada-US issues in government procurement. These include Buy American provisions and the small business "set-asides." This is how they work. In the United States, the Federal Government often provides funds to state and local governments requiring that the money be spent on suppliers and products that have a certain minimum proportion of US content. This is allowed under both the GPA and the NAFTA because it is not a direct purchase of the Federal Government that is covered by the Agreements. For example, the *Transportation Equity Act for the 21st Century* (TEA-21), which provides financing for transit, highway and airport projects carried out by state and local governments and private sector organizations, has Buy American provisions that require all steel and manufactured stock to be 100 per cent American content and all rolling stock to be 60 per cent American and assembled in the US.

The small business "set-asides" are Federal Government procurement preferences in the United States that reserve a certain proportion of government contracts for small business. These set asides are large, amounting to 23 per cent of the Federal Government's contract budget, and have usually been met or exceeded. And the US businesses benefitting are not so small either by Canadian standards, having as many as 500 employees in manufacturing (even 1,500 in some sectors) and revenue of up to US$17 million in services.

Without assurances that the United States will eliminate, or at least reduce, such discriminatory measures, the provincial governments have been unwilling to make commitments with respect to the procurement under their jurisdiction. These provincial government concerns are understandable. But, without the ability to commit provincial government procurement, the Canadian Government has come under heavy fire in the WTO Committee on Government Procurement for failing to deliver on its own commitments in its

Annexes 2 and 3 of the GPA to cover procurement under provincial jurisdiction. Canada's response to this criticism is that these commitments were conditional on getting commitments from the provinces, and, since no such commitments were received, there was no obligation to make an offer under these Annexes.

Regardless of who is right or wrong, the result is still the same: Canadian suppliers are deprived of preferred access under the GPA to the procurement market of sub-central levels of government in the other signatory countries. In addition, Canada's inability to get agreement from provinces to make procurement commitments is a major embarrassment that makes it difficult for the Canadian Government to provide the necessary leadership in the government procurement negotiations leading up to the Seattle Ministerial and that will undermine its credibility at the bargaining table.

The GPA has been important in opening up the large government procurement market of the major industrial countries to suppliers from other countries. Extending the Agreement to other, particularly developing, countries and improving its functioning is important for the future of the international trading system. The industrialized countries that are members of the GPA need to push harder to get developing countries, particularly the newly acceding countries, to join the GPA.

If Canada is to play a key role in negotiating a new strengthened Agreement on Government Procurement that will open up sub-central procurement markets in other countries to Canadian suppliers, the provinces need to be much more cooperative with the federal government. Only then will the Canadian Government be able to offer access under the GPA to provincial procurement in return for access to sub-central levels of procurement in other countries, including at the state and local level in the United States.

DISPUTES UNDER THE GPA

There have been three disputes under the new GPA. The first one dealt with Japan's procurement of a navigation satellite. On March 26, 1997, the European Community requested consultations with Japan regarding a Ministry of Transport procurement tender to purchase a multi-functional satellite for the installation of a navigation system for air traffic management. The EU complained that the specifications referred specifically to a US satellite based system called MTSAT Satellite-based Augmentation System (MSAS) and consequently discriminated against European companies that supplied another comparable system called the European Geostationary Navigation Overlay Service (EGNOS). Consultations resulted in a mutually agreed solution for the establishment of technical cooperation in the field of interoperability to produce a global seamless navigation system, thus ending the dispute. Requirements for interoperability will have to be mentioned in all future procurement starting in 1998, provided that it proves feasible.

The second dispute concerns the complaints of the European Union and Japan about a Massachusetts state law that prohibits state authorities and other state entities from procuring goods and services from anyone doing business with Myanmar (Burma), a country with a particularly odious human rights record. The request for consultations and the establishment of a panel was made in June 1997. As a US court case was underway, the panel did not report according to the normal timetable. In February 1999 following a US court ruling barring the implementation of the state law at issue, the European Union and Japan requested that the panel suspend its work. Unless the US court decision is overturned, the dispute appears to be resolved.

The third dispute, which was launched in February 1999 and is still underway, concerns the Korean Government's procurement practices in the construction of the new Inchon International Airport. More specifically, the United States contended that four particular practices were inconsistent with Korea's obligations under the GPA: requirements that prime contractors must have manufacturing facilities in Korea; requirements that foreign suppliers partner with Korean firms; the absence of access to challenge procedures; and bid deadlines that are shorter than the GPA-required 40 days. During the consultations, Korea asserted that the entities responsible for the procurement were not covered by the GPA. Consequently, in May 1999, the United States requested that a panel be established. The panel is now underway with an interim report due before the end of the year.

A fourth dispute relating to government procurement practices is also brewing. The United States is considering making a complaint against Japan concerning Japanese government construction contracts. It particularly irks the Americans that a Japanese company is building the new Los Angeles subway, while their construction companies are shut out of Japanese governmental markets.

The disputes show that governments are starting to exercise their rights and obligations under the GPA. At least for the countries covered, the Agreement is beginning to impose significant discipline on government procurement.

TRANSPARENCY IN GOVERNMENT PROCUREMENT AGREEMENT

In an effort to make government procurement practices more transparent, the United States proposed at the Singapore Ministerial in 1996 that a Working Group on Transparency in Government Procurement Practices be established. The purpose of this Working Group was "to conduct a study on transparency in government procurement practices, taking into account national policies, and based on this study, to develop elements for inclusion in an appropriate agreement." In contrast to the plurilateral Agreement on Government Procurement, this is a multilateral exercise aimed at achieving a WTO agreement on transparency. The intention was that the text of such an agreement could be ready for the Seattle Ministerial and that it could possibly be part of an early harvest of the negotiations.

The objective of an agreement on transparency is the worthy one of making certain that potential suppliers are provided with adequate information on the rules governing particular tenders. This allows suppliers to make an informed decision on whether or not to participate. This would save much wasted and frustrated effort by suppliers who never had a realistic chance to be selected under existing rules, but who didn't have enough information to know this in advance.

The information that would have to be published should at a minimum include: notices of procurement; policies and procedures; laws; evaluation criteria; contract awards; reasons for sole source procurement; bid challenge provisions for suppliers; and dispute settlement provisions for countries. While it is understood that a transparency agreement would not require countries to change preferential or discriminatory policies, at least it would make the rules clear for everyone.

The transparency agreement should apply to all levels of government, non-central as well as central. Again the Canadian Federal Government and the provinces, with the shared objective of increased transparency, need to cooperate if Canada is to offer a unified and credible front in the transparency negotiations.

A transparency agreement is a useful step in the direction of a multilateral Agreement on Government Procurement to replace the current plurilateral one. Once governments become accustomed to transparent procurement, it may not be as difficult to convince them to go the rest of the way to non-discriminatory procurement on a multilateral basis.

A transparency agreement will also help to combat corruption and related practices in government which is a big problem in some countries where government procurement decisions are often influenced by bribes or favouritism of one sort or another. The twenty-nine OECD countries have already entered into a Convention on Combating Bribery, which took force in February 1999. Under this Convention, OECD countries have agreed to cooperate in adopting and enforcing national legislation making it a crime to bribe public officials. This is good as far as it goes, but action also needs to be taken in the countries where the bribes are being received to make sure that the offending officials are punished.

Chapter 6

The E-Commerce Juggernaut

E-COMMERCE TAKES OFF

Electronic Commerce, which is defined is a 1998 WTO study as "the production, advertising, sale and distribution of products via telecommunications networks," has taken off for the stratosphere with the Internet. For what it's worth, the WTO estimates that by the turn of the century the value of e-commerce will have reached US$300 billion and international e-trade will represent 20 per cent of this or US$60 billion and growing. These are, of course, guesstimates. The only existing information on e-commerce flows is for the United States and a few other industrialized countries and data for cross border transactions simply does not exist. Needless to say, it always takes a while for statistics to catch up with reality, but as usual policy can't wait.

The potential for further growth of e-commerce is mind-boggling. Internet-based commerce, which currently accounts for only 2 per cent of all commercial transactions, is expected to swell to 50 per cent in ten years. The 13-percent share of consumer shopping currently conducted electronically is expected to more than double by 2007. The greatest potential for expansion is in financial services, telecommunications, advertising, travel, entertainment and professional services. But who knows for sure with such a new and revolutionary medium?

THE INCREDIBLE LIGHTNESS OF E-COMMERCE

E-commerce transactions have the same four stages as more conventional transactions – searching, ordering, paying, and delivery. For the commerce to qualify for an "e," at least some of its stages must be electronic. Usually, at a minimum, this includes ordering.

E-commerce is not only over the Internet. More mundanely, it also can occur over the telephone or fax. Just pick up the telephone and make an order. The delivery may be made in the traditional way of post or van, but it still counts as e-commerce. Much Internet-based commerce still relies on old-fashioned delivery methods.

ATM machines, which deliver banking services, are also a very specialized form of e-commerce. No one has yet figured out how to get currency into or out of a computer. But many banks offer Internet banking, which enables customers to pay bills and switch money from one account to another.

Professional services can also be delivered electronically. Architects and engineers can speak to clients over phones and send drawings and designs electronically. Doctors can provide diagnosis and prescribe treatment electronically. Accountants can prepare financial statements on line.

The quintessential form of e-commerce occurs on the Internet for digitalized products like software, books and music. All four stages of the transaction can be conducted electronically. The product can be ordered, paid for by credit card over a secure system, and downloaded electronically.

Internet-based commerce, like the Internet, is still in its infancy. It is the most exciting type of e-commerce, and is largely a US-based phenomenon with 85 per cent of Internet revenues generated in the United States. The pioneers are Microsoft, Dell Computer, Amazon.com, Charles Schwab, Home Depot, e-Bay, Realtor.com, E*Trade, Adauction, Chemdex, and NTE. You name it and they sell it over the net – software, computers, books and music, securities, building supplies, merchandise, real estate, advertisements, chemicals, transportation services. Even groceries and flowers are now being offered in the United States. And everyday something else is offered as "cybermalls" proliferate.

Canada is not far behind in e-commerce. Canadians are already accustomed to cross-border shopping. Making purchases in the United States is nothing new even if the medium is. Canada has also sprouted its own growing number of "virtual shops" on the web – Chapters.ca sells books, Corel.com software, and HMV.com music.

The best part of Internet shopping is that you don't even have to take your hands off the keyboard or get out of your ergonomically designed chair to find the lowest prices and the best products or to make a purchase. And no fossil fuels are burned and pollution created, other than the small amount required to generate the electricity necessary to power the computers.

With Internet-based commerce, all you have to do to open a shop is construct a web page, subscribe to a secure and reliable payments system, and set up a system for ordering and delivering purchases. The computer will replace many salespersons and shop clerks. The costs are much lower than for a traditional retail store. The potential size of the market is enormous, reaching 300 million PCs with Internet access. This will enable many small and medium-sized businesses to participate in international trade for the first time.

Internet-based commerce is spurred by lower transaction costs such as search costs, delivery time and charges, and travel and transportation costs. Internet search engines can tirelessly search out the lowest prices.

Consumers outside the US, and particularly those in high-income industrialized countries, have watched the emergence of Internet-based commerce through their computer screen with growing fascination. This has not gone unnoticed by their suppliers who are hastening to join the Internet revolution before their customers disappear in cyberspace along with their revenue.

The same advantages of the Internet that spur domestic e-commerce also foster international e-commerce. The Internet makes international advertising and price comparisons possible just as it does domestically. It also reduces transportation costs for digitalized products to zero, making formerly high-transportation-cost international suppliers competitive for these products. On the internet, consumers can buy digitalized products anywhere in the world and have them delivered almost instantaneously for free.

THE MORATORIUM ON CUSTOMS DUTIES

The United States, which has a massive comparative advantage in e-commerce and is probably the only country with a whopping surplus in e-trade, is understandably the champion of free trade in digitalized products. On February 19, 1998, it presented a proposal to the WTO General Council calling for an agreement among WTO Members "to maintain... current practices not to impose import duties on electronic transmissions." The United States and the EU had earlier reached an agreement on December 5, 1997 "to work together towards a global understanding, as soon as possible, that: (i) when goods are ordered electronically and delivered physically, there will be no additional import duties in relation to the use of electronic means; and (ii) in all other cases relating to electronic commerce, the absence of duties on imports should remain."

In its May 1998 "Declaration on Global Electronic Commerce," the WTO General Council agreed to establish a comprehensive work programme to examine trade-related issues relating to e-commerce" and to "continue ... current practice of not imposing customs duties on electronic transmissions." The moratorium on customs duties will be reviewed at the Seattle Ministerial in the light of the results of the work programme. It is important that this moratorium be transformed into zero bound tariffs on e-commerce and become a permanent feature of the international trading regime. This dynamic sector must be allowed to flourish and make its full potential contribution to the global economy.

GATT, GATS OR WHAT?

E-commerce doesn't fit neatly into one of the WTO's boxes. Goods like books and music CDs that are ordered electronically but delivered physically across the border are covered by the GATT and all the usual customs duties and procedures apply. But if they're digitalized and delivered electronically, there are no duties.

Computer software can also be delivered electronically. But there is no tariff on computer software because of the Information Technology Agreement. The only duty is on the value of the disk or CD containing the software. Thus the issue of different treatment of electronic and physical delivery does not arise.

Some e-commerce such as for professional services could be covered by the GATS if it falls under any of the specific commitments made by countries to provide national treatment. These commitments can vary depending on mode of supply. Is the acquisition of professional services from abroad "cross-border supply" or "consumption abroad?" The answer to this question can make the difference between gaining market access and being denied if the commitment is only with respect to one mode.

On a theoretical level, it's not obvious whether the delivery of digitalized information over the Internet should be considered trade in goods or in services. Some types of e-commerce have a permanency like goods. Others are intangible.

Whether e-commerce is trade in goods or in services is important because it determines whether it should be covered by the GATT or the GATS. There are important distinctions between these two agreements. As noted above, the GATT covers cross-border supply of goods and governs tariffs, whereas the GATS covers cross-border supply of services, the consumption of goods abroad, natural presence and commercial presence. The GATT provides for general national treatment, while the GATS provides only for specific national treatment commitments. The GATT has a general prohibition against quantitative restrictions, whereas the GATS permits Members to limit market access. If e-commerce were to fall under the GATT and be subject to zero tariffs, it would have much more liberalized market access than it would under the GATS. Nevertheless, because of the widely different characteristics of some of the transactions falling under the rubric of e-commerce, it is unlikely that it will be possible to develop one overall regime for this rapidly growing new form of international trade. Various WTO bodies are looking into these issues and will report on their conclusions at Seattle.

LEGAL AND REGULATORY ISSUES

Regulatory principles that were accepted by the signatories of the WTO Telecommunications Agreement and the GATS Annex on Telecommunications provide the required access to the telecommunications network to carry out e-commerce. This is important in establishing the interconnections necessary for the growth of e-commerce.

The Internet is still the wild, wild west. There are not yet laws and regulations for Internet-based commerce; these will have to be developed. But new laws, rules or regulations should not be any more restrictive than necessary. Complex legal issues must be resolved. For instance, which country's law applies, the buyer or the seller's? Are electronic signatures and documentation sufficient for a legally binding contract? To get the ball rolling, the OECD has proposed a uniform international commercial code for international electronic commerce.

For international e-commerce to take place, digital signatures and certifications must be interoperable across countries and internationally-accepted encryption methods must be available in all countries. The Secure Electronic Transactions (SET) Standard developed by two of the main credit card issuers meets these criteria. In this case, it's the private sector rather than the government that is providing the framework for e-commerce. While the Internet may have got its initial push in the late 1960s from the government in the guise of the Defense Department and the Advanced Research Projects Network in the United States, the emergence of the World Wide Web in the 1990s that led to the rapid expansion of e-commerce was a private sector development.

Governments will also inevitably want to regulate the content of the Internet. The WTO identifies three categories of regulation of e-commerce. The first seeks to prohibit or control content in the pursuit of universally-shared objectives such as the prohibition of child pornography or other information of a criminal nature. This type of regulation will have broad public support in most countries. The second category of regulation seeks to prohibit or control content deemed politically subversive by particular governments. There will be much less agreement about the appropriateness of this type of regulation because political objectives are not necessarily shared by other jurisdictions. The third seeks to protect consumers through licensing or qualification requirements and requirements for the provision of information. This type of regulations is also recognized as useful as long as it is not more restrictive than necessary.

Because of its unique and decentralized nature, the Internet will severely try the capacity of any one government, or even governments collectively, to regulate. Governments will have to rely on Internet users to regulate themselves to a much greater extent than has ever been the case for any other medium. This is not necessarily a bad thing as it will preserve the flexibility and innovativeness which is the Internet's strength.

The WTO, as the watchdog of the international trading system, is not in a position to judge the legitimacy of domestic regulatory objectives and their enforcement. However, there are two fundamental principles embodied in all the WTO agreements that it will need to ensure are respected. These are the "non-discrimination" and the "least-restrictive-trade" rules for regulations. The regulations should provide "national treatment" to make sure that foreign e-commerce suppliers are treated the same as domestic suppliers and should provide MFN treatment to make sure that foreign suppliers from different countries are treated equally. The regulations should also be specified so that they are no more trade-restrictive than necessary to achieve their objectives.

The WTO will also have to determine whether e-commerce constitutes "cross-border supply," "consumption abroad," or some combination of the two. This will have important implications for the national treatment commitments made under the GATS, if that is where e-commerce were to fall.

INTELLECTUAL PROPERTY

Much e-commerce is in products such as software and information that need to be protected by intellectual property rights. The TRIPs Agreement specifies that "computer programs, whether in source or object code, shall be protected as literary works." (Article 10:1). Other information including databases is also protected.

It's one thing to have an international agreement that provides protection for digitalized products like software, books, and music. It's another thing to enforce property rights in digitalized product when they can be reproduced at a zero cost and distributed across the web for free. Software piracy can be almost impossible to stop. An important issue in the Millennium Round will be to reach agreement on adequate enforcement mechanisms.

GOVERNMENT PROCUREMENT ON THE NET

Government procurement on the Internet is another kind of e-commerce. Governments are routing an increasing share of their procurement through the Internet because it enables them to reach the most suppliers and to get the best prices. It's also an easy way to meet the requirements for openness and transparency in the Government Procurement Agreement. The procurement section of the WTO website has hotlinks to all the member governments' procurement sites. As the GPA is modernized and streamlined, the web and e-commerce will play a much larger role.

FREE TRADE IN DIGITALIZED PRODUCTS

E-commerce has the potential to increase competition and consumer choice throughout the world. It also promises to be a powerful transmission mechanism for the new information technologies that will shape the 21st century. A key objective of the Millennium Round should be to preserve an environment free of tariff and quantitative restrictions for trade in digitalized products. If this objective is met, all of the other questions become secondary.

Chapter 7

Disciplining Subsidies and Antidumping

UNFAIR, UNSCHMAIR

When things start to go wrong in any trade relationship, it doesn't take long for at least one of the parties to accuse the other of unfair trading. This is much easier than having to admit that a competitor might have beaten us fair and square.

A case in point is government subsidization. Producers the world over naively believe, often despite much evidence to the contrary, that their own governments do not provide subsidies. On the other hand, they will steadfastly maintain that any success a foreign producer experiences is entirely attributable to support it receives from its home government. It is exactly this kind of reasoning that has given rise to a veritable arsenal of unfair trade instruments including countervailing duty actions. Worse still are domestic trade policies that permit governments to take unilateral action against perceived injustices in the trade arena.

Another tactic for intimidating "unfair" traders is to threaten an antidumping action. Dumping is trade-speak for when an exporter sells goods at a lower price in a foreign market than it charges at home, or at a price that does not cover the full costs of production. Up until recently, the United States and Canada were among the biggest users of antidumping actions. It was our dirty little secret. Now that new Members of the WTO have discovered this versatile and effective tool for restricting foreign competition, developed nations are thinking reform. The thought that a developing nation might end up passing judgement on whether our exporters are acting unfairly offends our own sense of fair play.

Pejoratives like "unfair" do not help advance the cause of trade liberalization much. Nor do such labels contribute to the predictability or certainty of the trading system. What is "unfair" to one party can seem perfectly "fair" to another. So far, it has been mostly in the eye of the beholder.

Clearly, good rules are needed to preserve the integrity of the international trading system. Firms that receive government subsidies and act in an anti-competitive fashion should be prevented from taking customers away from their competitors who play by the rules. By the same token, exporters themselves need to be guarded from ill-founded allegations of "unfair trading" that are merely a guise for plain old protectionism. Some progress was achieved in the Uruguay Round of trade negotiations, primarily in improving subsidy and dumping calculations, but much more remains to be done.

As with other areas of the trade agenda, negotiating objectives will have to be realistic. Some see trade remedies as the price we must pay for the tremendous progress achieved on other fronts, most notably in reducing tariff and non-tariff barriers. Countries might be more reluctant to abandon more traditional – and arguably, more damaging – types of protection if they believe that they will be left powerless to deal with unfairly traded goods that hurt their own producers. While there might be something to this argument, we should let someone else make it. Canada cannot afford to be too accepting when it comes to trade remedies. Not with the importance exports have to our economy. We must continue to take the high road and press for reform whenever we have the chance, beginning with the Millennium Round.

THE URUGUAY ROUND AGREEMENT
ON SUBSIDIES

The Uruguay Round made substantial progress in disciplining the use of trade-distorting subsidies. Moreover, in providing a mechanism to resolve disputes over unfair trade, it made the rules in this area much more enforceable.

The WTO Agreement on Subsidies and Countervailing Measures contains clear definitions of what a subsidy is. To be considered a subsidy, three conditions must be met:

- The government must either provide a financial payment or disbursement or it must forego revenue that is otherwise due;
- This must confer a benefit on the recipient; and
- The subsidy must be "specific" in the sense that it is provided to only certain enterprises, industries or groups of industries. Payments that are generally available, like unemployment insurance benefits are to all Canadians, would not be counted a subsidy.

It is not enough for a government simply to provide financial assistance. The government's action must be targeted in some way and must provide a verifiable advantage to the recipient. This ensures that only those subsidies that distort trade become the focus of WTO attention.

The Agreement then categorizes subsidies into three classes. Trade practitioners often use the traffic light metaphor of red, amber and green light subsidies as a characterization. Red light or "prohibited" subsidies are export subsidies and subsidies that are tied to local content requirements. Prohibited subsidies must be removed. At the other end of the spectrum are green light or "non-actionable" subsidies. Regional development, R&D, environmental and generally available subsidies are classified in the green category. All other subsidies fall into the amber category. Amber subsidies are "actionable" which means that they can be challenged if they cause material injury to the domestic industry of another Member in its own market or serious prejudice to the interests of another Member in a third country market.

The alternatives available to a WTO Member that wishes to challenge a foreign subsidy practice depend on the type of subsidy and the nature of the harm that it causes.

Prohibited subsidies – the most heinous kind of subsidies – are subject to abbreviated dispute settlement and enforcement procedures. If a measure is found to be a prohibited subsidy, the dispute settlement panel must recommend that the subsidizing Members withdraw the subsidy immediately.

Unlike the situation for red light subsidies where their mere existence only has to be established, amber light subsidies are subject to an injury test. Members who challenge an amber light subsidy first must demonstrate that the subsidy falls into the actionable category and, second, must show that it causes them economic harm. Economic harm is usually established by demonstrating that the subsidy caused prices to fall or sales to be lost to the subsidized goods.

Actionable subsidies can be subject to a countervailing duty action or to a serious prejudice action, depending on whether they affect a challenger's home market or whether they affect the challenger's sales into a third market. If subsidized imports cause material injury to domestic producers, a countervailing duty can be imposed.

Subsidized goods that are hurting sales into a third market can be challenged on "serious prejudice" grounds. This was an option open to Canada in challenging the Brazilian government's subsidy to its regional aircraft industry over the 1997-99 period. A countervailing duty action was out of the question since Canada was not importing the subsidized Brazilian aircraft itself. However, the Brazilian subsidy was displacing sales of the competing Canadian product into the US and European markets and causing serious harm in the process. In the end, Canada did not need to pursue a serious prejudice challenge against Brazil because the Brazilian subsidy fell into the prohibited category.

The Uruguay Round's other achievement was that it made disagreements over subsidies subject to the WTO's dispute settlement provisions. Generous allowance is made for consultations aimed at reaching mutually agreed upon solutions. However, if consultations fail, the end result is a final and binding determination. This gives the subsidies rules teeth.

THE CANADA – BRAZIL DISPUTE OVER SUBSIDIES TO REGIONAL AIRCRAFT

The recent Canada-Brazil battle over subsidies to regional aircraft provides an interesting glimpse into the workings of the WTO Agreement on Subsidies and Countervailing Measures.

Bombardier, the world's third largest civil aircraft producer has long been concerned about subsidies provided by the Brazilian government to its home-grown aircraft manufacturer, Embraer, Bombardier's chief competitor in the regional aircraft business. After years of arm-twisting, Bombardier was finally able to persuade the Canadian government to challenge the Brazilian subsidy programs at the WTO. What ensued was an ugly, hard-fought battle that, despite wending its way through all the WTO dispute settlement processes, may still be far from over.

What rankles Bombardier so is Brazil's PROEX program. PROEX provides a 3.7 percentage point interest-rate "buy down" to foreign purchasers of Embraer aircraft that, in the view of the WTO panel and supported by the WTO Appellate Body, constitutes a prohibited export subsidy. While Brazil maintains that PROEX is merely to overcome the disadvantages of being a developing country, in actual fact the subsidy payments are applied to the foreign buyer's own financing costs even if it already has a AAA credit rating. The PROEX subsidy can amount to some $1 million on the price of a $16 million aircraft. This provides Embraer with a massive advantage in the marketplace.

Outraged by Canada's challenge, Brazil launched an attack of its own. It charged that Canada subsidizes its aerospace industry and breaks a host of WTO rules in the process. The first government programme the Brazilians challenged was the Technology Partnerships Canada (TPC) program, a retread of the old Defence Industry Production Program (DIPP) that provides royalty-based financing to Bombardier, Pratt and Whitney and a handful of other high tech manufacturers. Brazil also complained that loans made by Export Development Canada and using Canada Account money to support aircraft exports amounted to prohibited export subsidies.

The WTO panel ruled that Canada's research and development assistance under the TPC program constitutes an export subsidy. In smaller economies like Canada's, high-technology industries can end up exporting virtually all of their production. This is the case for aircraft where the Canadian market is very small. Subsidies to these industries can, for all intents and purposes, look an awful lot like export subsidies, even though that was not the objective of the government in designing the programs. Annoying as this is, it is a relatively small matter to modify TPC to bring it into compliance with WTO requirements. Not so for PROEX, however, which was dealt a mortal blow by the WTO panel.

The Brazilians love a good fight and were not prepared to admit defeat on this one. We Canadians are a much more reticent lot and refuse to gloat, even in the face of victory. The WTO's decision was clear: PROEX must be immediately abolished, TPC must be fiddled with. Canada scored a big triumph at the WTO. Although, it was hardly portrayed that way in the press coverage of the WTO case.

Canada has to remain vigilant to ensure that we did not win the battle only to lose the war. Indications are that Brazil is busy finding creative ways to continue providing PROEX subsidies. The complexity of this type of market transaction and the level of secrecy required make it most difficult to keep track of what a competitor is doing. The WTO needs complete information to convict. Once burned, Brazil is unlikely to be as forthcoming in the future. Often, by the time the information is available, the sale is already lost.

The Canada-Brazil wrangle and other recent disputes over subsidies have highlighted some shortcomings in the WTO rules. These will have to be addressed in the next round of negotiations.

THE FOREIGN SALES CORPORATION CASE

Tax breaks can also constitute export subsidies under the SCM Agreement. This was underlined by a WTO panel decision released in July 1999 on an EU challenge of the US Foreign Sales Corporation (FSC) program. Under this program, US corporations, including such giants as Microsoft and Boeing, get a 64-per-cent corporate tax reduction on profits earned by offshore subsidiaries on exports of goods that have a high level of US content. These subsidiaries are located mainly in the Virgin Islands, but also in Barbados and Guam. The Foreign Sales Corporation is a major incentive estimated by the EU to cost the US Treasury US$2 billion per year. The EU charged that this tax reduction constituted a prohibited export subsidy and gave US goods an unfair price advantage in foreign markets. The panel agreed and ordered that the program be abolished before October 1, 2000. This was the same fate as a predecessor program called the Domestic International Sales Corporation (DISC) suffered at the hands of a GATT panel in 1976. Apparently, the changes to the program were not sufficient to make it WTO-consistent.

The United States has long complained that European Value Added Taxes, which are rebated on exports, provide an unfair advantage for European companies competing with American on international markets. The Foreign Sales Corporation tax benefit pales beside the magnitude of these taxes. These grumblings have intensified following the loss of the FSC case. The US has never challenged the EU on the VAT, but if it were to do so it would make for an interesting case, raising interesting public finance issues about the legitimacy of a destination versus an origin basis for indirect taxation. Canada with its GST would have much at stake in the resolution of the issue.

SUBSIDY ISSUES FOR THE MILLENNIUM ROUND

The Uruguay Round left many subsidy issues for the next round of negotiations. By far the most important is the question of agricultural subsidies which was discussed in detail in Chapter 3. In terms of industrial subsidies, the Agreement on Subsidies and Countervailing Measures calls for a review of its provisions on amber and green light subsidies. This provides negotiators with an opportunity to strengthen the subsidy disciplines by expanding the list of actionable subsidies.

The next round of negotiations also provides a chance to address issues related to notification, transparency and enforcement. The more we know about the programmes in place in other WTO countries, the less potential there is for trade-distorting practices.

DUMPING ON ANTIDUMPING

The last round of trade negotiations left the decades-old antidumping code essentially intact. While some important changes were made to improve administrative practices, particularly in calculating the amount of duties that can be applied, the highly protectionist instrument remains very much alive and well.

Economists do not think much of antidumping measures. To them, it is quite natural for firms to want to price differently in different markets. It is just a case of adapting to local competitive conditions. When demand is weak, it also makes sense to sell goods at less than fully allocated costs. This sort of thing is done all the time within a national market. What is perfectly normal behaviour for firms operating in their home markets is potentially illegal for exporters. If foreign firms engage in these practices, they can be hit with dumping duties and driven out of import markets. Inevitably, it is the consumers and domestic users of the dumped product that pay the penalty for the protection in the form of higher prices.

There are some situations where there is a legitimate justification for putting a stop to dumping. One such situation is when predatory pricing is occurring and the exporter is intent on destroying domestic producers to gain a monopoly for itself. Unfortunately, the antidumping regime is poorly equipped to determine whether an exporter's actions are really predatory in nature. Most competition regimes, including those in Canada and the United States, would do a much better job.

Another situation where antidumping protection is justified is to deal with the effects of trade restrictions in the dumper's home market. Occasionally, import restrictions prevent the normal process of arbitrage that works to equalize prices between the exporter's and importer's market. This arose, for example, when the Canadian sugar industry was swamped by low-cost dumped and subsidized sugar imports from the United States and Europe in the early 1990s. The US essentially prohibits imports of refined sugar. What's more, Europe and the US provide generous subsidy programs and price support schemes that generate massive surpluses in production. The surplus sugar entered Canada in vast quantities, threatening to destroy the Canadian industry. Canadian refiners could not retaliate by exporting sugar into the US or Europe to take advantage of high prices there. The only option was to pursue a countervailing duty and antidumping case.

Arguably, the US and Europe should never have been able to support their domestic sugar growers in such a trade-distorting fashion. Sadly, however, the agricultural area is one where trade rules are still very permissive. Unless and until better rules are developed to discipline the harmful combination of import restrictions and domestic price support, antidumping actions will remain a weapon that many WTO Members will be unwilling to relinquish.

The truth is that few antidumping actions can be justified on the grounds of predatory pricing or import restrictions in the exporter's home market. Most are examples of simple protectionism. The prospect of being hit by an antidumping complaint is terrifying to exporters. Just ask the Canadian steel industry about the millions and millions of dollars they have spent in the past decade defending themselves in US courts and administrative tribunals.

To say that the gains from trade are not fully realized when an antidumping regime is in place is a massive understatement. What then is the alternative?

SAFEGUARDS

One possibility for steering WTO Members away from using antidumping actions is to encourage them to pursue safeguard cases instead.

Safeguard or emergency actions are another form of trade remedy. As trade remedies go, however, they are somewhat less atrocious. Unlike countervailing and antidumping actions, Members pursuing a safeguard case do not need to prove that the imports were traded unfairly. All that has to be established is that import volumes have been so high or increased by such an extent that they are causing serious injury to the domestic industry. If so, some kind of temporary import restriction can be imposed.

The trouble is that WTO Members do not much like safeguard actions. Safeguard actions have a higher injury standard than do antidumping actions. Since more "hurt" has to be demonstrated, it is harder to put safeguards into place. Also, the WTO Agreement requires countries imposing safeguards to compensate the exporting country.

Members will not substitute safeguards for antidumping actions unless changes are made to the Antidumping Agreement to make it less appealing to use. One possibility would be to raise the injury standard. Another would be to make the antidumping protection more temporary. A number of other refinements could be made to the system which would have the effect of lowering the protective duties. There are many options available to pursue, if the will exists.

COMPETITION POLICY OFFERS SOME HOPE

Competition laws in most developed nations are well-equipped to deal with situations of predatory pricing and abuse of dominant position, "lawyer-speak" for monopolists behaving badly. The good thing about competition policy measures is that their preoccupation is with protecting the state of competition, not with protecting domestic producers per se. Freeing markets from anti-competitive influences should mean lower prices and more choice for consumers.

In the Canada-Chile Trade Agreement, the two countries agreed to suspend the use of antidumping measures on bilateral trade and to rely on competition law instead. This example notwithstanding, an "internationalized" competition policy regime is probably too far-fetched an alternative to antidumping, at least for the time being. The best evidence of this is that even Canada and the United States cannot agree to pursue the idea seriously.

What are the prospects for multilateral reform if even Canada and the United States, despite our similar regimes and harmonious bilateral relationship, refuse to dump antidumping measures between us? The answer is not very good.

Many WTO Members have quite rudimentary competition regimes. Some lack them altogether. Until Members have confidence in their own regimes and those of their trading partners, we will be stuck with antidumping.

Competition policy is an important new item on the Millennium Round agenda in its own right. Work is already underway to better coordinate competition policy regimes internationally. The OECD has an active work plan in this area. The WTO Working Group on Trade and Competition has been busy selling the message to developing countries that competitive market structures are conducive to growth and wealth creation. Canada is engaged in discussions with a number of countries on cooperation and information exchange. Competition policy measures already form part of some WTO Agreements, notably the Agreement on Basic Telecommunications.

The multilateral game plan is very long term in nature. The idea is to start slowly by affirming the basic principles of transparency, national treatment and most-favoured-nation. Next, efforts will be made to promote better cooperation and communication through the sharing of information and through technical cooperation. Ideally, measures to encourage WTO Members to enforce their own competition laws would be desirable, as would some dispute settlement mechanism. Down the road, more ambitious objectives, such as harmonization and replacement of antidumping regimes might be tackled.

Lasts Words on Trade Remedies

We will probably never be entirely rid of unfair traders or of those who unfairly hound their trading partners on that basis. The only hope for lessening the effects of unfair trade is to address the issue on several levels. First, we need stronger disciplines on the use of unfair trade measures such as subsidies. This accomplishes two objectives. First, it reduces the use of trade-distorting practices which is good for the integrity of the international trading system. Second, stronger disciplines might make it easier to convince Members to weaken or even abandon their use of trade remedies. The argument is that better policing of unfair trading practices will make the high-powered weapons both unnecessary and downright dangerous to leave lying around.

At the same time, we need to promote the idea of competition policy as a replacement regime for antidumping measures – the least endearing of all the trade remedies. The odds of actually achieving this on a multilateral level are remote at best, certainly in the short term. However, better coordination and cooperation in the use of competition laws is a worthwhile objective in its own right. The high degree of interplay between trade, investment and competition issues make it a natural in terms of Millennium Round priorities.

Canada should never lose its sense of innocence and determination when it comes to reforming the global use of trade remedies. Despite being both a charter Member and a frequent flyer of the antidumping and countervailing duty club, the truth is we been more hurt than helped by trade remedies. We should be prepared to gladly curtail our use of antidumping measures in exchange for the United States' agreement to do likewise. Getting the rest of the world on-side would be an added bonus. If our negotiators aim high in this area, we might live to see the realization of their efforts.

Chapter 8

The Return of the MAI

THE SPECTRE AT THE TABLE

Our research has yielded no support to rumours that federal trade negotiators admit to having recurring nightmares featuring Maude Barlow, Chairperson of the Council of Canadians, in a starring role. But there is no denying that the rift between the prospective deal-makers and the representatives of "civil society" is vaster when it comes to trade and investment than it is for any other area.

Despite the resounding defeat of the MAI initiative within the OECD, WTO Members, in a fit of masochism, have signaled a willingness to consider negotiations on investment in the upcoming Millennium Round. This support remains pretty lukewarm at present. Even the US, which is widely credited with championing the "corporate agenda" on foreign investment, has signaled that it considers it an open question whether a modest package on investment could be included in the WTO talks. Clearly, the objective is to tread carefully in this mine-infested area.

If talks do proceed, negotiators can expect spirited opposition worldwide from non-governmental organizations who are buoyed by their self-proclaimed success in killing the MAI. Any progress on the investment file will depend on winning over these powerful opponents – a difficult challenge indeed. It will also mean crafting a deal that will bridge the interests of developed countries intent on drafting clearer rules to protect foreign investors with the desire of developing country Members to resist the prospect of foreign domination.

THE LINKS BETWEEN INVESTMENT AND TRADE

Global stocks of foreign direct investment (FDI) reached US$3.5 trillion in 1997, a 23 per cent increase over the previous year. Increases in FDI have significantly outpaced the growth in international trade in recent years, continuing a fundamental international economic trend that has characterized the 1980s and 1990s.

Foreign investment has rather a bad reputation in certain circles. It conjures up visions of greedy young men in red suspenders creating havoc for developing – and even developed – nations. Notwithstanding the exhortations of Malaysian Prime Minister Mahathir, however, foreign investment flows are an essential facet of today's business environment. In a world of transnational organizations, strategic firm alliances and world product mandates, investment policy can matter as much or more than conventional trade policy. Foreign investment leads to the transfer of technology, ideas and best practices between global enterprises. It increases wealth and employment and acts as a conduit for the transfer of goods and services. It provides a way to access foreign markets in spite of trade barriers.

Groups like the Council of Canadians have made a name for themselves preaching against the evils of foreign investment. The fact is that foreign capital has been an essential part of Canada's economic achievements since our very beginning as primarily a fur and fish trading nation. It has paved the way for many of our industrial successes, not the least of which is motor vehicle production, our number one sector in terms of employment and trade. Far from making us beholden to foreign masters, inward foreign direct investment has contributed importantly to Canada's strength and independence as a major economic power.

Preferring to portray Canada as the perennial victim though, the Council of Canadians would rather ignore the fact that Canada is now a net exporter of investment capital worldwide. In 1997, the stock of FDI in Canada was estimated to be $188 billion, less than the $194 billion Canadians invested abroad. This subtle but significant shift reflects our coming of age as a economic player and underlines the critical links that bind us to the global economy.

Bombardier's success in foreign markets provides an excellent illustration of how outward investment can benefit Canadians. Bombardier has grown from its origins in a small Quebec town to a world leader in the field of transportation. It now ranks as the third largest civil aerospace manufacturer in the world, the second largest manufacturer of passenger rail and mass transit car equipment and a global leader in the recreational products area with its highly successful Sea-Doo and Ski-Doo vehicles. More than 90 per cent of the companies revenues of over Can $11 billion are generated in markets outside of Canada. Significantly, 42 per cent of its 50,000 employees are located in Canada.

Investment in foreign markets has been central to Bombardier's strategic success. The company now operates plants in 12 countries. Establishing a local market presence has been particularly important in the mass transit business because of local requirements for a customized product and government procurement practices favouring domestic suppliers. Foreign investment has permitted Bombardier to sell a Canadian product to foreign markets, generating jobs here at home.

THE CASE FOR MULTILATERAL RULES
ON INVESTMENT

Critics of negotiations on trade and investment maintain that it is all part of an underhanded plot by multinationals to force their corporate agenda on unsuspecting governments. Clearly, international standards proscribing what is fair and not fair when dealing with foreign investors would help the business community. What is less apparent, but equally compelling, are the gains that would flow to developing nations and to taxpaying citizens the world over from a liberalized investment regime.

First, the corporate agenda. Most multinational companies can provide chapter and verse on investment restrictions they encounter in international markets. The obstacles can be as seemingly innocuous as the measures instituted by developed nations to restrict foreign ownership in strategic sectors like broadcasting, banking or resource development. In the developing world, foreign investors can be outrightly prohibited, forced into joint ventures with local firms or coerced into dealings with local authorities that lead to the transfer of funds, technical expertise or a variety of other favours.

One common scenario is something like the following: an exporter of manufactured goods is told that in return for access to a foreign market, it must establish a local commercial presence. In addition to the costs of constructing and operating a plant that might well be superfluous to its business needs, the company has to put up with many capricious demands from local authorities. To address domestic concerns over foreign investment, it is told that the plant must be established in a specific location, in partnership with a local business person and that it must employ local contractors and engineers and purchase its materials from local suppliers. Even with these conditions met, the investor is not home free. It faces a constant threat of expropriation or other forms of interference by government officials.

Foreign investment restrictions increase operating costs for businesses. The costs are both out of pocket and the costs that come from delays, uncertainty and from the inefficiencies that arise from building smaller than optimal plants in less than desirable locations and operating them according to somebody else's rules. Multinational companies have come to accept restrictive investment regimes and work around them. Many have employees whose sole task is to understand and provide what makes local officials happy. Sadly, once they reach this point, multinationals can become advocates for the retention of investment restrictions as a means of keeping competitors out of their favourite markets. This, more than anything, should convince us of the need for a liberalized investment regime.

Stronger rules governing trade and investment might not be all gravy for the business community. One area where multinational corporations will not be leading the charge for reform is in the area of investment incentives. As taxpayers, we shake our heads at the way companies shop from jurisdiction to jurisdiction looking for the most generous package of tax breaks, grants and other hand-outs when deciding where to locate a plant. Japanese car manufacturers are adept at squeezing every last goodie out of states, provinces and municipalities when contemplating the construction of factories in North America. New Brunswick's former Premier Frank McKenna was renowned for his tendency to pull out the cheque book whenever he got into a conversation with business interests, even within hearing range of his fellow Premiers on Team Canada trade missions in Asia.

When governments pay companies to locate in their jurisdiction, it costs the taxpayer money and it makes poor economic sense. Quite often, these businesses fall short of achieving their true potential because they were enticed somewhere where the business fundamentals just don't add up. They ultimately pay a price in terms of competitiveness which costs the economy as a whole.

But the benefits to developed countries like Canada of a freer investment regime pale in comparison to the advantages that would flow to the developing world. An open and predictable climate for investment would bring needed capital and know-how to developing countries. Evidence strongly supports the fact that FDI improves wages and living standards, particularly in low income nations. Foreign investment provides one of the best means for disadvantaged nations to better their economic circumstances.

Prime Minister Mahathir of Malaysia was quite wrong in blaming foreign investors like George Soros for his country's financial crisis. His real problem lay much closer to home. If investors have more certainty that local regimes would not yield to drastic measures like capital controls and expropriation during times of economic hardship, they would be much more inclined to keep their capital in place and weather the economic storms. This provides far better insurance than exchange controls and other restrictions do in averting an economic crisis.

It is exactly for these reasons that the IMF and World Bank, in the wake of the recent Asian Crisis, are encouraging countries to liberalize their investment restrictions as a condition for assistance.

CANADA'S INVESTMENT AGREEMENTS WITH OTHER COUNTRIES

Largely unnoticed in the spectacular interest surrounding the MAI is the fact that Canada has already signed onto a number of investment agreements. In addition to the NAFTA provisions governing investment contained in Chapter 11 of the Agreement, Canada has bilateral Foreign Investment Protection Agreements (FIPAs) with over twenty countries.

CANADA'S BILATERAL FIPA PARTNERS		
Poland	Argentina	Hungary
Costa Rica	USSR	Ukraine
Philippines	Barbados	Venezuela
Egypt	Armenia	Latvia
Trinidad & Tobago	Ecuador	Panama
Thailand	South Africa	Croatia
Uruguay	Romania	Lebanon
Czech & Slovak Republics		

The NAFTA Chapter 11 and FIPA provisions are more or less the same. All contain the following key elements:
- most-favoured nation commitment to treat foreign investors from the signatory country no less favourably than other foreign investors;
- national treatment provisions ensuring that foreign investors are treated on an equal footing with domestic investors;
- rights to transfer funds freely and without delay;
- rules on expropriation, including compensation;
- permission for foreign investors to have free choice in senior personnel;
- disciplines on performance requirements (such as domestic content rules and technology transfer requirements) imposed on foreign investors;

- the right for governments to adopt environmental measures consistent with the principles of the agreement;
- a commitment to keep government policies towards investors transparent; and
- provisions for the resolution of disputes, both state-to-state disputes and investor-state

Canada has negotiated special treatment for sensitive sectors in these agreements. We are able to implement policies in the cultural, social, health and education field that might otherwise run afoul of the commitments made in Chapter 11 of the NAFTA.

FIPAs may provide Canadian investors protection, but their geographic coverage is far from complete. There are 135 Members of the WTO, yet we only have twenty-two agreements. Simple mathematics reveals why bilateral agreements are a cumbersome and imperfect substitute for a multilateral agreement. Full coverage for all the WTO countries would require 9,045 separate treaties when one would suffice.

WTO INVESTMENT RULES

Investment rules also form part of existing WTO agreements. The Agreement on Trade-Related Investment Measures (TRIMs) prohibits some performance requirements (such as domestic sourcing and export restrictions) in some goods-producing industries. The General Agreement on Trade in Services provides for the "right of establishment" for foreign service providers wanting to establish a commercial presence and commits Canada and other WTO Members to provide non-discriminatory treatment to specified service industries. Coverage of the TRIMs and the GATS Agreements is limited, however. In the case of the former, only goods are covered. In the latter, only service sectors where countries have made commitments are subject to disciplines.

Canada has already made far-reaching commitments in the investment area, particularly with respect to US and Mexican investors under the NAFTA. Why then does the prospect of an investment pact with other WTO Members cause such concern? One would think that the payoff, in terms of gaining easier access for our investors to foreign markets, is greatest in the multilateral arena.

THE MAI DEBACLE

Negotiations aimed at reaching a Multilateral Agreement on Investment were launched in the Organisation for Economic Co-operation and Development in 1995. The OECD, which is a 29-member association for developed nations, proposed that the MAI be a free-standing agreement open to both OECD and non-OECD Members. The objective was to achieve a comprehensive framework providing high standards for liberalization and investment protection and a system for resolving disputes.

It did not take long for members of the NGO community to zero in on what the OECD was up to. Web sites were established, fund raising drives launched and book deals signed. Groups such as our own inimitable Council of Canadians proclaimed that negotiators were creating a bill of rights for multinational corporations. The result, they maintained, was that governments would be powerless to set their own social, environmental, cultural and health policy without challenge from foreign companies. The horror stories and scare tactics were spectacular and, quite often, blatantly false.

Unfortunately, in an area as complex as investment finance, the patriotic message of those opposed prevailed over the more complicated but reasoned arguments of the advocates. There really was no contest. Canadians were convinced that Maude Barlow loves her country more than do our captains of industry and trade policy officials.

It is an interesting question, though, whether the NGO crowd really did defeat the MAI. Their self-congratulations aside, there is ample reason to believe that the MAI was doomed at birth even without their interventions.

In the first place, the forum was all wrong. Sure, it is usually easier to reach an agreement on just about anything among "like-minded" countries of the OECD, but investment is different. The truth is that investors from OECD nations do not have trouble doing business in other OECD nations. The difficulties lie elsewhere, notably in the developing world. Consequently, for multinational investors there was no real upside to an investment pact among rich nations, at least not enough to put up with the heat inflicted by opponents to the MAI back at home. Better to wait until there is an agreement worth fighting over.

Second, indications are that MAI negotiations got bogged down over other substantive issues. Matters such as culture caused serious problems for the negotiations. Further, a concern arose over the ability of member nations of the European Union to maintain autonomy in the negotiations. France, for example, shared Canada's interest in safeguarding culture and wanted to strike out on its own in this area.

It's not clear whether governments have learned anything from the MAI fiasco. They certainly are keeping a low profile on upcoming negotiations. This is smart. The last thing they need is to spook domestic opponents into generating a groundswell of resistance so early on. The success of the entire Millennium Round depends on keeping as many domestic constituencies as possible on side and committed to the benefits of trade liberalization.

A "WISH-LIST" FOR A MULTILATERAL PACT

With the MAI defeat so fresh in our minds, what is the best strategy for success in the Millennium Round? The answer lies in aiming for the achievable. The focus should be on the big prize: a pact with developing country members and their implicit recognition that foreign investment is a positive force in helping them to realize their economic goals.

As such, a multilateral investment agreement should do little more than affirm the principles of national treatment, transparency and most-favoured-nation. Indications are that developing countries are the most resistant to granting "rights of establishment" to foreign multinationals. This is understandable given their history of domination by the East-India and United-Fruit-type companies of this world. Hence, it might be most realistic to limit ourselves to rules governing the treatment of existing investors in this round of negotiations. Disciplines on the use of performance requirements would also be desirable as would some code of conduct in cases of expropriation. Assurances will have to be provided with respect to the sovereignty of member governments in sensitive areas such as environment, culture and social policy.

Investment is one area where the WTO can act in concert with its two Bretton Woods sisters in advancing the interests of the developing world. The IMF and World Bank can play an important role in convincing developing nations of the folly of measures such as exchange and capital controls. There is no reason why the WTO should be left taking all the heat on the trade and investment file.

Another element that would be desirable to include as part of a multilateral investment pact is a set of disciplines governing the granting of investment incentives. Taxpayers the world over would rejoice if their governments would agree to cease and desist in the bidding war game to give away money to corporations. While the likelihood of ever achieving meaningful multilateral disciplines on investment incentives in this round is slim, it shouldn't stop us from continuing to ask our corporations and governments for rules in this area in the hope that they might finally see the light.

Canada is poorly suited to claim a leadership role in negotiations on investment incentives. We have strongly resisted any attempts to have provinces and municipalities bound by multilateral commitments and it is at this level where most investment incentives are granted. Notwithstanding disciplines in the Agreement on Internal Trade, provinces continue to open their pocketbooks to almost any investment opportunity that comes calling. That is why multilateral agreements are so important. They save countries from costly mistakes made by their governments.

INVESTOR-STATE: ARE THE CRITICS RIGHT?

Most of what the critics say about investment pacts are dead wrong. They might be on to something in their criticism of investor-state dispute settlement, however. It is conspicuously absent from our wish-list of desirable provisions for a multilateral pact as it is from the Japanese and European negotiating positions on investment.

Under the investor-state obligations of the NAFTA's Chapter 11 and Canada's FIPA bilaterals, foreign investors who believe that a government regulation or policy has reduced the value of their investment are entitled to "sue" the government for compensation.

A recent example is the NAFTA challenge brought by The Loewen Group Inc., a Canadian-based funeral home and cemetery business, against the US government in late1998. The claim seeks compensation for a $500 million jury verdict in Mississippi in an earlier breech of contract case. Loewen was effectively prevented from appealing the Mississippi case because of requirements to post a $625 million bond – a condition it considered excessive and punitive. The company is maintaining that it was subjected to "discrimination, denial of the minimum standard of treatment guaranteed by NAFTA and uncompensated expropriation, all in violation of NAFTA."

Loewen's worthy quest aside, there are a couple of problems with investor-state provisions that trouble even the most hardened free-traders. The first is that they can undermine a government's sovereignty to conduct legitimate domestic policy and regulatory initiatives. As such, they can end up undoing exemptions negotiated as part of trade agreements in areas such as social and environmental policy.

The other big problem with investor-state provisions is that they treat foreign investors better than domestic investors. Most countries in the developed world safeguard the rights of investors in situations of expropriation by providing compensation at market rates. Very few jurisdictions formally extend the same privilege to investors who retain ownership of their property but suffer a reduction in its value because of government action.

Negotiators might be well-advised to tread carefully in the area of investor-state when crafting multilateral rules on investment. Developing countries might find these rules particularly hard to swallow, especially since they already make policy-makers in the developed world uneasy.

EXTRA-TERRITORIALITY

The extraterritorial application of one country's laws to another is a hot topic at the WTO that has found its most controversial application with respect to investment. The worst offender is the United States with its Cuban Liberty and Democratic Solidarity (LIBERTAD) Act (more commonly known as Helms-Burton) and the Iran-Lybia Sanctions Act.

The Helms-Burton law, which permits US citizens to sue foreign companies making use of properties expropriated in these countries (Title III of Helms-Burton) and allows the government to deny visas for executives and shareholders of companies doing business there (Title IV), is designed to punish Cuba by discouraging foreign investment. While the US Administration has regularly suspended the right to sue under Title III, liabilities have still been accruing. Canada and Mexico have been subject to sanctions for trading or investing in Cuba under Title IV. Canadian businessman, Ian Delaney, the Chairman of Sherritt International and several other senior executives have been banned from entering the United States because their company has been using facilities confiscated from Freeport-McMoRan of New Orleans. Canada has passed its own Foreign Extraterritorial Measures Act to try to shield Canadian companies from Helms-Burton.

The Iran-Lybia Sanctions Act requires the US Administration to impose sanctions on foreign firms that invest more than $20 million a year in the energy sectors of the two countries. The US government further antagonized an EU already upset over Helms-Burton with its threats to penalize the French oil company Total for its plans to invest $2 billion in the Iranian gas sector.

The EU launched a WTO case against the US for its extraterritorial application of economic sanctions in October 1996, but suspended the challenge for a year in an effort to reach a settlement. Under the terms of the April 1998 deal, the US agreed to suspend sanctions against multinational companies doing business in Cuba, Iran and Libya; and the EU promised to discourage investment in these three countries by prohibiting governments from providing financial aid to companies that break the US law against investing there. This agreement does not really permanently resolve the problem of the extraterritorial application of US laws as they remain in force and can still be enforced. But it was the best that the EU could get in the circumstances. The EU knew that nothing good would come from pursuing the dispute through to a final panel decision. The US was already boycotting the panel on the grounds of the "national security" exception in Article XXI of the GATT, and had indicated that it would refuse to submit to any ruling on the same grounds. This would have undermined the credibility of the whole dispute settlement mechanism, which was something the EU definitely did not want to do.

A related dispute involving the EU has just cropped up and more talks are underway. The EU is complaining that a US law known as "Section 211" violates the WTO TRIPs Agreement. Section 211, which prohibits the recognition in the US of trademarks confiscated by Cuba, was invoked by a US court in a lawsuit over the ownership of the Havana Club label to deny Havana Club Holding, which is owned jointly by Pernod Ricard and a Cuban company, the right to use the brand in the United States. The court ruled that under section 211 the label belongs to Baccardi, which obtained the required consent from the original owner of the brand, the Jose Arechabala family. The EU has threatened to take this case of the extraterritorial application of US law to the WTO. The issue of extraterritoriality of US economic sanctions has clearly not been resolved and is also likely to come up in the Millennium Round.

WHITHER GOEST INVESTMENT?

Who really knows what the on-again-off-again investment negotiations will generate by way of a multilateral pact? Member countries are understandably reluctant to show their hand at this stage for fear of igniting the fires of opposition back at home. Despite their coyness, expectations are that negotiations will proceed as part of the next round of negotiations. Member countries of the WTO know that success in the trade and investment area is important to continuing the momentum of liberalization, given the tremendous interplay between capital and trade flows in today's global economy.

The chances of success in the Millennium Round depend on keeping expectations in check. The best outcome would be a deal that includes developing countries, however modest its contents. Successive rounds can tackle the harder elements such as universal rights of establishment and curbs on investment incentives. In light of these humble expectations, Canada should have little trouble safeguarding its sensitive sectors like culture, especially since our concerns in this area are shared by other WTO Members. By all rights, investment negotiations ought to give critics like the Council of Canadians little to bay about. But that won't stop them from campaigning bitterly against any agreement, thus ensuring that negotiations on investment will be one of the most eventful in the upcoming round.

Chapter 9

Protecting Intellectual Property

INTELLECTUAL PROPERTY AND TRADE

The ancient Greeks used to preach that knowledge is power. But even those clever Greeks could not possibly have imagined how strong the link would turn out to be between technological know-how and global prosperity. Today it is truer than ever that those who control the ideas end up holding all the cards.

Protecting ideas has become an important trade issue. The WTO Agreement on Trade-Related Intellectual Property (TRIPs) formally brought the setting of standards and the enforcement of intellectual property rights into the multilateral arena. Possible extensions to the TRIPs Agreement will be one of the most contentious areas of the Millennium Round, one that is certain to accentuate the divisions between the developing and developed world.

One might well ask what the protection of ideas has to do with trade liberalization? Indeed, protecting intellectual property rights can end up restricting competition and trade – something one would think the WTO would want to avoid. Ultimately, though, companies are more likely to export to and invest in other economies if they are satisfied that their products and processes will not be pirated. The argument is that trade will expand, along with the technology that accompanies it, if intellectual property rights are enforced worldwide.

Cartoon by Stuart Carlson © *Milwaukee Sentinel* 1999. Reprinted with permission of Universal Press Syndicate. All rights reserved.

What are Intellectual Property Rights?

Intellectual property rights are the entitlements that are granted to individuals or companies for their original creations. Ordinarily, intellectual property rights give the creators exclusive rights to use their creations for a specific period of time.

There are two main branches of intellectual property with two quite different sets of concerns. The first is copyright which applies mostly to literary, musical, artistic, photographic and audiovisual works. In recent years, the coverage of copyright has been expanded to computer programs and data bases. It has also been broadened to include "neighbouring rights" which extend property right protection in the sound recording industry from the composers and lyricists to producers and performers as well.

The second branch is loosely coined industrial property. It can be further sub-divided into two areas. One is chiefly concerned with protecting signs of various sorts – trademarks and geographic indications (which are names for goods that are based on the location where the good is produced. Examples include "Champagne" and "Cognac"). The second area of industrial property rights is primarily concerned with inventions, innovations and the creation of technology.

THE WTO TRIPS AGREEMENT

The WTO certainly did not invent intellectual property. The concept of patent, copyright and trademark protection at the international level has been around for at least a hundred years. The Berne Convention, which protects copyrights, was originally signed in 1886. The World Intellectual Property Organization (WIPO), which provides a forum for negotiating and administering various treaties on intellectual property, was created in 1967. Like many similar international organizations, however, the WIPO lacks provisions to enforce its treaties and obligations.

Although raised toward the end of the Tokyo Round, intellectual property protection was successfully negotiated for the first time at the Uruguay Round. The TRIPs Agreement obliges all WTO Members to enforce its minimum standards by implementing them in their domestic legislation. While developing Members were given a generous time frame for implementation, developed nations had only one year to incorporate into domestic law the proper kind of administrative and criminal procedures to make intellectual property rights fully enforceable.

The TRIPs Agreement also makes disputes over intellectual property matters subject to the WTO's dispute settlement system. There have already been a handful of disputes over intellectual property issues including the European Union's current challenge of Canada's patent protection of pharmaceutical products. The EU maintains that Canada violates the requirements of the TRIPs Agreement because it offers patent protection for a 20-year period, which commences with the date an application for patent is filed. According to the EU, the 20-year protection period should begin once all the regulatory approvals have been granted, which might be as long as several years after the original patent application was made.

There is a great deal of interplay between the TRIPs Agreement and a variety of other intellectual property treaties that are administered by the WIPO. The TRIPs Agreement requires WTO Members to adhere to provisions of a variety of international conventions governing intellectual property including *The Paris Convention for the Protection of Industrial Property*, *The Berne Convention for the Protection of Literary and Artistic Works* and the more recent *Treaty on Intellectual Property in Respect of Integrated Circuits*.

All of the seven target areas in the TRIPs Agreement (see box) must adhere to the basic principles of national treatment and most-favoured-nation. The Agreement establishes a set of minimum standards for intellectual property in certain specific areas.

The TRIP Agreement's Seven Target Areas for Intellectual Property Rights
• copyright and neighbouring rights;
• trademarks;
• geographical indications;
• industrial designs and models;
• patents;
• layout designs of integrated circuits; and
• protection of undisclosed information (the TRIPs term for trade secrets).

Several of the TRIPs Agreement's provisions bear special notice. Article 27 of the Agreement requires Members to make patents available without discrimination for any inventions, products and processes, in all fields of technology. The patent period is typically 20 years. Certain exceptions are permitted under strict conditions.

The Agreement excludes patents on higher forms of life such as whole plants and animals, although it gives discretion to individual Members in this area. The United States, Europe and Japan are among those that do allow patents on higher life forms. Canada does not as yet. The Agreement's provisions on biotechnology are to be reviewed in the next set of negotiations. This is certain to be one of the most controversial areas of discussion and possible negotiation.

It is still early days for the TRIPs Agreement since many countries still have time left to implement its obligations. It remains to be seen whether it will achieve its stated purpose.

COPYRIGHT

Although we might be reluctant to admit it, we have probably all been guilty of breaking copyright laws in one way or another. Photocopying excerpts from a textbook, copying a friend's CD onto a cassette tape or recording a favourite television show on our VCR all qualify as unlawful duplication. However, this is penny ante stuff compared to the possibilities for piracy that the new technologies provide. The prospect of musical or artistic masterpieces being downloaded free from the Internet greatly concerns those in the cultural community. This is just one example of the scope for unauthorized reproduction, publication and transmission available in the digital age.

It is difficult to find anyone who does not believe that people should be prevented from stealing the creative inventions of musicians, writers and other artists. Artists need the protection of copyright in order to support themselves through their artistic efforts. Otherwise, we will have potential Picassos washing dishes for a living. Clearly, we would far rather see Alanis Morrisette properly rewarded for the music she creates than toiling in the Ottawa bureacracy to make ends meet.

The trouble is that it is virtually impossible in this age of technological sophistication to prevent unlawful duplication of cultural works. Short of banning the sale of CD burners and restricting access to the Internet, a government's options are few. The issue becomes one of finding a way for all users to compensate the creators and artists for the possibility that some users might steal from them.

Many do not like the mechanisms imposed to ensure fair compensation for artistic products. A case in point is the criticism that has accompanied the special tax imposed on blank cassette tapes and compact discs sold in Canada. The idea was to use the tax proceeds to compensate composers and musicians for infringements in their intellectual property rights.

The TRIPs Agreement requires WTO Members to adhere to the Berne Convention. The Berne Convention applies to books and other written works, musical compositions, film works and various artistic works. The TRIPs Agreement added computer programmes and compilations of data to the Convention's scope. The Convention requires Member countries to protect the works for the life of the "author" and for 50 years after his or her death.

The copyright provisions of the TRIPs Agreement are adequate but could do with a bit of updating. The Canadian Recording Industry Association maintains that all WTO Members should ratify two 1996 treaties of the World Intellectual Property Organization dealing with copyright, performance and phonogram issues. The treaties update the standards and legal principals governing copyright in the electronic age. Canada has begun the process of ratifying and implementing the WIPO treaties itself.

PROTECTING INDUSTRIAL PROPERTY

The far more complicated issue is that of protecting industrial property. It raises fundamental questions of fairness and entitlement that are not easily resolved in the international context.

The two sides of the debate line up as follows. The so-called "multinational viewpoint" which is advanced by US and EU negotiators, is that strong enforcement of intellectual property rights is essential for the innovation process.

Unless inventors are confident that their ideas will be protected and rewarded, they will be unwilling to undergo the time-consuming and expensive process of research and development that is so beneficial to the economy and to society as a whole. It follows that countries that vigorously enforce intellectual property rights make themselves better locations for inward investment. This was the argument used to justify Canada's patent drug legislation.

The US and EU perspective has a number of detractors, beginning with developing country nations. They wonder why they are expected to pay so dearly for ideas that originate in the developed world, especially when these ideas would dramatically improve the well being of their citizens. A case in point is the drug regime used to treat AIDS, a disease that is devastating Africa. The AIDS cocktail that has been effective in treating patients in North America is prohibitively expensive and beyond the means of most African residents and nations. The South African government has passed legislation that would allow local pharmaceutical companies to manufacture imitation AIDS drugs in defiance of the patents that exist in the US and Europe. South Africa is certain to incur the wrath of its powerful trading partners, in spite of its noble intentions.

These sort of strains exist even within developed nations. Groups such as the Friends of Medicare point to the high percentage of Canada's overall health care costs that are accounted for by patented pharmaceuticals. Shortening the drug patent period from its current 20-year term would give cheaper generic drugs earlier access to the market. The savings in health care costs could be considerable. Tempting as this might be, the government made important commitments on patent protection to the brand-name drug industry in return for scores of jobs in Montreal ridings.

The other problem with vigorous patent enforcement is that the current trend is to patent anything that moves. The prospect of patenting human genes or rain forest bio-diversity is positively repugnant to some, especially since the source of the patented substances – remote aboriginal communities or rain forest dwellers – could end up paying to access to their own material. The advent of new biotechnologies and genetic materials complicate the issue even more.

Intellectual property protection is both the cause of and the solution to some of the problems in the developing world. Inventors and scientists give the problems of the developing world scant attention. While the best pharmaceutical brains in the world have dedicated themselves to improving the sex lives of well-healed Westerners through medications like Viagra, millions of children in Africa die from malaria and other potentially preventable diseases. The sad truth is that a malaria vaccine would never pay for two reasons. The first is because its likely customers are impoverished. Second, without patent enforcement, any effective vaccine that was developed would be quickly pirated.

This same imbalance in priorities applies to research aimed at improving agricultural yields. Crops grown in tropical nations are neglected in favour of the needs of farmers in temperate zones. The fact that seed varieties are being patented at a furious pace, taking them out of reach of the developing world, makes developing nations even more frustrated.

Developing countries are painfully aware that they lack the necessary knowledge and technology to adequately provide for their citizens. They view the intellectual property right system as somehow limiting their access to this knowledge, perpetuating a world of "haves" and "have nots". This is the perspective that they are likely to bring to Seattle and later to Geneva.

HARD CHOICES FOR THE MILLENNIUM ROUND

What is a poor Canadian IP negotiator to do? On one hand, groups like the Business Council on National Issues urges Canada to insist that creators of intellectual property have adequate incentives and effective protection. This position is also advanced by the US and Europe whose multinationals offer the enticing prospect of jobs and investment to those countries that offer safe havens for patented technologies. To ignore the implicit threats of powerful research-intensive companies is to play a dangerous game indeed with Canada's economic prosperity.

The Canadian government is also getting pressure from generic drug manufacturers and others to loosen the stranglehold multinational corporations have on the instruments of wealth creation. Concerned Canadians are raising important questions about the ethics of patenting some of the things that are being patented these days.

Issues such as artistic copyright and trademarks are straightforward; the fruits of the artistic process should be protected to ensure that pirates do not divert proceeds away from genuine creators. Efforts should be made in the WTO to ensure that the rules pertaining to copyright fully capture the potential offered by today's electronic wizardry. Diana Krall should be the one making most of the money from her CD sales, not some bootlegger. Nike and Gucci should be free to charge exorbitant sums for running shoes and loafers bearing their logos, not counterfeiters.

For other areas of intellectual property, some global navel-gazing might be in order. First, serious questions should be asked about the scope of patent protection. Unless and until we have thought through the ethical and practical implications of patenting such things as biotechnologies, genetic products, indigenous heritage, and perhaps even seeds and vaccines, we should resist efforts to extend the TRIPs Agreement to cover these items.

Second, we must be highly sensitive to the views of those in the developing world. Intellectual property is an area that breaks very much on developed – developing country lines. There is some scope for compromise, if developed countries are up to it. One possibility would be to offer a shorter period of patent coverage in developing countries for those products that are essential to their basic development needs. Another is for multinational companies to undertake to fund a certain amount of basic research in developing countries on issues of importance to the developing world, in return for patent protection on other products.

For their part, developing countries need to acknowledge that some form of intellectual property protection would enhance their own interests. Many of the advanced products and processes that developing nations regularly use in the telecommunications, transportation and health area would vastly improve the quality of life in the developed world. However, unless some basic level of patent protection is granted, they could very well remain outside the reach of the nations that they would benefit most.

The challenge of intellectual property both domestically and internationally is to achieve a fair balance. Innovators need to be rewarded with intellectual property protection but there may be good and valid reasons for limiting this protection in some instances. Economic prosperity depends on the creation of good ideas. At the same time, these ideas need to be easily and efficiently diffused if we are to improve the well-being of our world community.

Chapter 10

Defending Culture

FINDING COMMON GROUND

Sheila Copps knows better than anyone of the painful nexus between culture and trade. As Minister of Canadian Heritage, she has been known to holler more than once at trade policy bureaucrats who have tried to curb her passionate zeal. While the serious guys in suits have won the most recent trade policy battles, the odds are that Sheila is just taking a temporary breather to lick her wounds. She's certain to be back and raring to go – just in time for the Millennium Round.

The interesting thing about disputes over trade and culture is that many of the problems are entirely preventable. They arise not from any fundamental issues inherent in the Agreements or with Canada's policy objectives but with an inability of those within the trade community to understand the world of culture – and vice versa. Two solitudes as self absorbed as those of culture and trade diplomacy are hard to find. It is little surprise that the debates have been conducted on such different planes and with such scant success.

It does not help that events in the trade and culture file unfold under a microscope. The very *raison d'être* of cultural industries is to inform and entertain the general public. They are the media, or they have excellent access to it. Consequently, when cultural industries come under attack through a trade challenge, they meet it in the best way they can, by defending their position on the airwaves and in magazines and newspaper columns. In one sense, this is good because Canadian culture is important and should be protected. However, it can leave us with the impression that fights over culture are the only ones that matter. It can also lead to the oversimplification of issues which makes for bad policy-making.

Cultural issues are complicated ones to solve. Sometimes it is even tough to express opinions about them. It is an area where one has had to establish one's bona fides before weighing in. The audience has to be assured that the commentator loves Canada more or at least as much as the next person and is willing to stop at nothing to protect our culture. Trade consultants wanting to mine the cultural field are well advised to have a Can-lit or artistic icon as an immediate family member. Otherwise, they need not even bother hanging up a shingle.

Of course, this is all rather silly. What we need for Canadian culture is less blather and more strategy.

Culture in Canada

Describing Canada's cultural sector is made difficult by the fact that few people even agree on a definition of culture. Some consider culture to be an ubiquitous, all encompassing thing like our shared values and beliefs. The nationalists among us think the only culture that counts is Canadians talking to other Canadians. Economists tend to view culture more narrowly as a product or service that is produced by an identifiable industry and can be paid for and consumed in the same way as any other. To technocrats, culture is defined by the medium that is used to deliver it – the airwaves, the sound waves, the printed page, the electronic message. Divergent as these perspectives are, the one common theme is that culture has important non-market dimensions.

While one should avoid making generalizations about Canada's cultural sector, a couple of observations are in order. The first is that Canada is very open to foreign cultural influences. The following statistics underline this point:

- foreign books account for 45 per cent of book sales in Canada;
- 81 per cent of English-language consumer magazines on Canadian newsstands and over 63 per cent of magazine circulation revenue are accounted for by foreign titles;
- foreign-produced films represent 85 per cent of the revenues from film distribution in Canada; and
- some 95 per cent of screen time in Canadian theatres goes to foreign (mostly American) movies.

Hollywood has a strangle-hold on our imaginations, not to mention our pocketbooks. A high proportion of what we read, hear and watch, particularly in English-speaking Canada, is fed to us from a foreign producer.

It is impossible to generalize about Canadian culture. Our culture can be high-brow as in the Royal Winnipeg Ballet or the Vancouver Symphony. It can also be as low-brow as the Tom Green show. Canada boasts of some immense cultural successes like Shania Twain and Céline Dion who operate in the global big leagues. Indeed, our own "Lord-in-Waiting", Conrad Black, counts as one of the world's leading media moguls. At the other end of the commercial spectrum are cultural producers that could not survive without Canada Council funding. They are the present-day equivalent of the starving artist in the garret studio.

The fact that we deal with two rather distinct cultural communities makes it more complicated to devise good trade and cultural policy. One facet of our cultural sector is export-oriented, technologically up-to-date and quite comfortable in the global marketplace. The other is geared to the domestic market. It is the one most concerned about talking to Canadians about Canada and other Canadians. While this division is hardly unique to Canada, our proximity to the American cultural powerhouse has unnerved us more than most. We need to find ways to preserve that segment of our cultural sector that reminds us of who we are and what we share. At the same time, we must avoid clipping the wings of those who would fly wide and high to bring us acclaim, and export revenues, in world markets.

CULTURE AND TECHNOLOGY

To borrow the refrain from a once-popular song, has video killed the radio star? When last we checked, radio is still around but it and other traditional cultural vehicles are under serious attack from new technologies.

Technology have always been an issue for the cultural sector. One only has to think of the introduction of "talkies", mechanized printing presses, recordable phonographs and VCRs to appreciate the constant adaption made by the industry over the years. Indeed, to shield the cultural sector from technological advancement would be both fruitless and misguided. Culture has to be exposed to the upheavals of technological change if it is to stay inspired, relevant and connected to its users.

But the current technological revolution is bringing change at a whirlwind pace. The Internet has made cultural products vastly more accessible but much harder to protect and control. Consumers in Canada can read magazines and newspapers from all over the world. We are not nearly as bound by time, location, nationality and financial resources in our enjoyment of cultural products as our parents and grandparents were.

As new technologies extend the range of cultural works well past their traditional boundaries, it becomes much harder for governments to promote their domestic cultural sectors with the same box of policy tools. Internet versions of newspapers and direct-to-home satellite transmissions are but two examples. In earlier days, when governments wanted to protect domestic broadcasters they would grant licenses to domestic players only and they would impose a series of conditions on what programs could be broadcast and when. With home satellite and Internet broadcasts, regulators have lost much of their control of the airwaves.

The split run magazine case that found its way to the WTO is another example of how technology has undermined governments' ability to restrict foreign cultural products. Canada used to impose a prohibitive tariff on imported magazines. In an effort to get around this tariff, American publishers started to beam versions of the magazine by satellite to publishers located in Canada to be printed here. The idea was that since the magazines were no longer physically crossing the border, there was no product to be taxed or denied entry. The Canadian government met this development with a special excise tax imposed on split-run magazines, a tax that was eventually shot down by the WTO. The next technological wave promises to be even more illusive, however. New electronic versions of reading material and other cultural products can be beamed directly to the home and customized with articles and advertizing that is geared to the individual reader's interests, income level and demographic profile.

This is not to say that new technologies will make it impossible for countries to protect and promote their cultural sectors. They do make it much harder though. In their quest for new policy tools to protect indigenous culture, a worldwide preoccupation, governments might be well advised to do some collective brainstorming.

HOW CANADA PROMOTES AND PROTECTS ITS CULTURAL SECTOR NOW

If you believe the Reform Party's culture critic, Canada's cultural policy is preoccupied with grants to the creators of dumb-blonde joke books and art exhibits comprised of rabbit carcasses. In fact, this is only the tip of the iceberg.

Canada uses three basic instruments to protect its cultural industries: financial support in the form of subsidies and tax measures; Canadian content regulations; and foreign ownership restrictions.

Canada has a long, long list of government programs that provide financial support to the cultural sector. In addition to Canada Council grants to publishers and (dwindling) financial support to the CBC, there are a host of special programs aimed at the sound recording business, the video and television industry and the multimedia sector. New funds are being established on a regular basis to meet the needs of emerging technologies.

Over time, the structure of public support has gradually shifted away from pure cash subsidies to loan guarantees, equity investments and tax credits. An example is the Canadian Television Fund, a Can $200 million vehicle for equity investment in TV programming.

Financial assistance to cultural producers also comes in the form of tax relief. To support Canadian broadcasters, the Canadian Income Tax Act permits advertisers to deduct the cost of ads they place with Canadian stations but limits the deduction for ads placed with American broadcasters. Similar tax provisions apply to Canadian businesses taking out advertisements in newspapers and magazines. Canadian film and video producers are eligible for tax credits on their production costs.

The second basic instrument – Canadian content regulations administered by the CRTC – are considered to have been among the most effective vehicle for advancing our cultural sector. While best known is the requirement that radio programming reserve 30 per cent of its broadcast time for Canadian products, 'Can-Con' regulations also apply to TV programming, and to distribution systems including cable and Direct-to-Home satellite. Essentially all broadcasting systems are expected to provide Canadian programming and make a financial contribution to Canadian content.

The final instrument available to government is foreign ownership restrictions. They are based on the premise that Canadian-owned distributors, broadcasters and publishers are more likely than their foreign-owned competitors to disseminate Canadian content. While an arguable proposition, it is not going to be true in all instances.

The Investment Canada Act allows the government to review any foreign investment in almost any cultural industry to determine its net benefit to Canada. Depending on the sector, additional restrictions can also exist, including performance requirements of various sorts. For example, a film distribution policy enacted in 1988 limits any new foreign film distributors operating in Canada to distributing only those films that it has produced or controls itself. The fact that this restriction was "grandfathered" and does not apply to American distributors who were already in the Canadian market angered Polygram, the huge Dutch distribution giant. However, the EU turned the other cheek and did not pursue a trade case against Canada, less because of the merits of the case and more because Polygram ended up being bought by the Canadian corporate powerhouse, Seagram.

Restrictions also apply in the book retailing business that limit foreign owned companies from selling books as their primary activity. In the broadcasting area, only companies with more than 46.7 per cent Canadian ownership and de facto control by Canadians are granted licenses by the CRTC.

Many of the policies used to promote the cultural sector in Canada offend, if not the letter, at least the spirit of our WTO obligations. Other programmes and policies are no longer effective because technological advances have rendered them powerless or redundant. Canada is far from the only country in this position. The next round of WTO negotiations could not be coming at a more interesting time for the cultural sector.

THE TRADE RULES GOVERNING CULTURE

Despite the best efforts of the US negotiating team in the Uruguay Round, culture occupies a very small place in the WTO Agreements. In fact, its absence is rather conspicuous.

As Canada discovered first hand in the WTO case over magazines, how cultural measures are treated in the WTO Agreements depends very much on whether they fall under the General Agreement on Trade in Goods (GATT) or the General Agreement on Trade in Services (GATS). This creates much uncertainty since deciding whether a cultural creation like a sound recording or a film is a good or a service is a difficult proposition at the best of times. Sadly for Canada, the magazines dispute was not one of our best times.

With two minor exceptions, the cultural sector is subject to all of the standard disciplines encompassed in the GATT including the basic principles of most-favoured-nation and national treatment. The first of the exemptions falls in Article IV which permits countries to establish quotas for the exhibition of films. This is in recognition of the longstanding European practice of maintaining screen quotas. Second, Article XX allows exemptions from general GATT principles for measures aimed at protecting national treasures of artistic, historic and archeological value.

In the GATS, culture is almost nowhere to be seen, despite hectic efforts right up to the dying days of the Uruguay Round to hammer out an agreement on audio-visual services. Canada requested and was granted an MFN exemption for the film and television treaties we have with a number of countries. Moreover, we failed to make any commitments whatsoever on national treatment in the cultural sector. It is likely that our reticence will not go unnoticed in the next set of negotiations, particularly since the GATS Agreement is one that has been singled out for further liberalization. Canada will be under pressure to include in its GATS schedule commitments to provide national treatment to foreign investors and exporters of some cultural services.

If the Americans have much to say about it, the next round of negotiations will probably focus on resuscitating the failed audio-visual services negotiations and expanding the list of commitments under the GATS Agreement. Culture will also enter into other negotiating areas including intellectual property, e-commerce and investment. The existing TRIMs Agreement prohibits performance requirements as a condition of foreign investment. However, the current Agreement covers only certain sectors, and culture is not one of them. Culture would be hard-pressed to escape unscathed from any comprehensive agreement on investment.

For Canada, the most significant trade issue arises not from the WTO Agreements, per se, but from how they were interpreted in the recent trade challenge over magazines. The consequences of this has already had profound implications for how we conduct cultural policy in this country.

THE BIG FLAP OVER MAGAZINES

Before getting into the specifics of the WTO case over split-run magazines, it is useful to understand where the US is coming from on culture in general. American entertainment giants like Jack Valenti and Ted Turner believe that culture is really just a business like any other. In fact, entertainment is big business in the US, ranking second behind aerospace in terms of export activity. Not only do cultural exports generate lots of economic wealth in their own right but they are a vehicle for the promotion of a whole host of other US-produced goods and services, everything from Coca Cola to the Ford cars the X-Files stars drive around in. Some cynics even see cultural exports as part and parcel of the dissemination of American values and ideas throughout the world.

Of course, the US cultural sector has a soft underbelly just like ours. The National Endowment for the Arts is only one of a long list of well-heeled public benefactors. Chances are that US public sponsors might even have the odd meat dress, Voice of Fire and rabbit carcass skeletons in their own cultural closets.

The point is that the United States has taken an ambitious and aggressive attitude towards trade and culture. It has displayed little patience towards the efforts of countries like Canada, France and Belgium to restrict access to American cultural exports, viewing such attempts as simple protectionism.

The Canadian magazine industry has long been concerned with split-run products entering from the United States. A split-run is a magazine with predominantly US editorial content that is supplemented with Canadian advertisements. Canadian publishers fear them because split-runs siphon off lucrative advertising revenue which is the source of the majority of their revenue. Moreover, the fact that most of the costs of the US publications is covered in the larger American market means that they can offer cut-rate deals to Canadian advertisers and subscribers.

In December 1995, the United States launched a WTO challenge of three Canadian measures aimed at protecting our magazine industry from its split-run competitors. The first measure that the US challenged was a tariff code that prohibits imports of split-run magazines. The second measure attacked was an 80 per cent excise tax on advertising revenue earned by split-run publications Finally, the US challenged a postal subsidy programme, the effect of which was to allow Canadian publishers to put a cheaper stamp on magazines they mailed to subscribers than their split-run counterparts.

Canada lost conclusively on magazines. It was a bad sign when the WTO panel refused to accept our argument that magazines and their embodied advertising constitute a service as opposed to a good and should be governed by the more lenient GATS. With respect to the import prohibition on split-runs, the panel's decision was straightforward: such prohibitions violate a number of trade provisions and are not permitted. The panel went on to decree that Canada's excise tax discriminated against US imports, thereby violating the GATT's national treatment provision.

Concerning the postal subsidy, the WTO ruled that any subsidy that is not granted directly as a payment to domestic producers violates the GATT rules. This was easy to fix in this instance – Canada now gives postal subsidies directly to Canadian publishers – but the decision might have implications for other cultural industries that indirectly benefit from subsidies to others.

Of course, it could have been much worse for Canada. Luckily for us, the US chose not to challenge the provisions of our Income Tax Act that allow Canadian businesses to deduct the cost of advertising in Canadian, but not foreign, publications and television and radio stations. This was rather handy because by the time the WTO panel and Appellate Body had finished with us, the income tax provisions were the only policy we had left to support our magazine industry.

The panic that greeted the WTO decision caused a lot of flailing around in the Canadian culture and trade communities. Officials at Canadian Heritage proposed Bill C-55 which would have made it illegal for Canadian businesses to advertise in split runs. Their logic was that in focusing on advertising, a service, the policy would fall exclusively under the laxer GATS provisions and could avoid getting caught by the WTO. The US thought that we were trying to be too cute by a half. It saw the Bill as an outright attempt to avoid implementing the WTO's determination. To turn up the heat, the US threatened to retaliate against a handful of very well connected industries including steel and textiles. An all-out trade war seemed imminent.

Cooler heads prevailed in the end. Canada and the United States entered into negotiations over the amount of Canadian advertising a foreign publication should be allowed to have. The result was an agreement that up to 18 per cent of advertising revenue can be generated from Canadian sources without the magazine having to add any Canadian editorial content. The agreement allows American publishers to establish wholly-owned subsidiaries in Canada to publish Canadian editions as long as the editions contain a majority or substantial amount of Canadian content. Canada also instituted a new subsidy scheme for magazines worth an estimated $90 million per year. The subsidy provided to individual publishers will be based on a formula determined by lost advertising revenues and postal subsidies.

Many in the cultural community believed that Canada was unwise to capitulate to the US in the magazines dispute. They viewed it as part of a slippery slope towards total cultural domination by Washington. Canadian culture is something they consider worth standing up for notwithstanding the cost. At least we should not give up before the first shots are fired they say.

Important as our cultural sector is, Canada cannot afford to flout international trade rules. The cultural sector cannot reasonably expect another Canadian industry to pay the price for its refusal to meet our international trade obligations. There are other ways to support our cultural sector that do not violate trade principles. We need to explore these.

In the end, Canada had to accept the WTO decision. We must rely on our status in the international trading arena and use the system to change the system. That means better rules for culture that will help us avoid the kind of mess we got into with magazines.

Cartoon by Anthony Jenkins, *Globe and Mail*, May 22, 1999. Reprinted with permission of the *Globe and Mail*.

TO EXEMPT OR NOT TO EXEMPT?

Many in the cultural community steadfastly maintain that culture should be off the table in any trade negotiations. A blanket exemption for culture is the minimum deal they would find acceptable. Their belief is that had such an exemption been in the WTO Agreements, as it is in the NAFTA, we would never have lost the magazine dispute.

Is the exemption route the best strategy for promoting and protecting our cultural sector? Probably not.

The NAFTA's supposed exemption for culture is not as good at it seems at first glance. What it allows is for Canada to pursue policies towards the cultural sector that might not be consistent with other aspects of the Agreement. They might violate the principle of national treatment, for example. However, in such situations, the United States is entitled to take measures of equivalent commercial effect. This means that Canada must pay a price for cultural policies that violate the basic provisions of NAFTA. The price is usually paid in the form of trade retaliation against some other sector of the Canadian economy. And one can bet that a favourite target for retaliation is an industry like steel that is based in the hometown of the minister responsible for Canadian culture.

Of course, this must sound rather familiar to those acquainted with the WTO case on magazines. The WTO rules allow a Member who has successfully challenged another to take "appropriate countermeasures," to equivalent commercial effect, if the losing Member does not comply with the WTO panel and Appellate Body report. If Canada lost a challenge to one of our cultural policy measures and we refused to change the policy to comply with the WTO ruling, the challenger could retaliate against another of our industries.

Essentially then, the NAFTA exemption is worth little more than the WTO's non-exemption. In fact, it may be worth less. The WTO rules require the Dispute Settlement Body to formally authorize countermeasures and to determine what the appropriate level should be. The situation could get much messier under the NAFTA. The United States could decide on its own accord to retaliate against one of our cultural policies and could unilaterally decide on the retaliatory action it wanted to take. In such circumstances, Canada could end up fighting with the US for years over whether our cultural policies violated the NAFTA in the first place and whether the countermeasures implemented by the US were appropriate.

In truth, the NAFTA never really did exempt culture. The suggestion that it did was just slick marketing by those anxious to sell the deal and the FTA that preceded it. The NAFTA's cultural exemption is little more than permission to break the rules on the understanding that the US could retaliate in kind against some other industry. This is more or less the same deal we have in the WTO.

Okay then, the cultural pundits might argue, we should seek an unconditional exemption for culture in the WTO. Canada has negotiated such provisions in the bilateral foreign investment agreements that we have signed with various countries. They provide a carte blanche exemption for investment policies for the cultural sector and do not allow for retaliatory countermeasures.

We might, however, want to think this through. The first question to ask is whether our cultural sector could live with the kind of restrictions that a blanket and unconditional exemption would impose. Consider that culture is an ubiquitous and expansive phenomenon. Countries could decide that a whole host of things impact negatively on their culture – things like processed cheese, polyester neck ties, or country music – and attempt to block their importation. Alternatively, a country could determine that having a national aerospace industry or a world-class wine industry is essential to its national cultural identity and generously subsidize these ventures, distorting world trade in the process. While far-fetched, these examples underscore a critical point. Unless we put some limitations on what is and what is not considered culture, the very idea of an unconditional exemption should be out of the question.

It is also important to remember that if Canada were to get an unconditional exemption, so too would other WTO Members. That might not sit well with some elements of our cultural sector, particularly those which depend on export markets. Canadian television shows sell all over the world. It's a good thing too, since TV shows are dreadfully expensive to produce and foreign revenues make many of these productions possible. Our national pride swells at the thought that Margaret Atwood is enjoyed by readers in many foreign lands. Having her books restricted to our tiny market would take away much of our fun, not to mention our stature on the world cultural stage. But a cultural exemption is a cultural exemption. We would have no leg to stand on if our trading partners decided that our cultural products should be denied a place in their markets.

It does not take too long to see that a cultural exemption is an acceptable notion but only if we define culture precisely and provide some guidelines on the types of instruments that could be used to protect it. In fact, what we are talking about is rules for culture as opposed to exemptions for culture.

WHAT THE CULTURAL COMMUNITY SUGGESTS

An obvious place to start in preparing for the negotiations is to take stock of what the cultural community suggests. The trouble is that many of the statements that the cultural experts make just do not get us very far. Consider the declaration that "culture is not a commodity like any other." While there is no disputing this, the same could be said of a lot of products, not to mention services, that are the subject of international negotiations. There is no doubt that culture is a highly distinctive area. But we are still better off in the end to engage our trading partners in rational discussions about culture instead of making conversation-stopping statements that mean almost nothing.

The trouble is that some of the basic myths are questionable. One dominant myth is that globalization is bad for culture and for cultural diversity. Quite apart from the fact that there is little evidence to support this claim – indeed, there is evidence to the contrary – it is a misleading notion. The very idea of protectionism should be anathema to culture. After all, culture depends on the spontaneous and unrestrained flow of creative ideas. That, not the desire to protect and shield, should be our basic point of departure.

Another challenge that the cultural experts set out for trade negotiators is to affirm the importance of cultural diversity. Affirmations, in themselves, mean very little and therefore are pretty harmless. It is probably better this way. For this affirmation to mean something would be to create a potentially damaging outcome. We must not give our trading partners the tools to deny us access to their markets, at least not unless we fully realize what we are doing and get something in return.

A final observation concerns the special cultural instrument recommended by the Cultural Sectoral Advisory Group on International Trade (SAGIT). While the specifics are lacking, the thought is a constructive one. It makes imminent sense for WTO countries to try to agree on the kinds of domestic policies that should and should not be used to enhance cultural and linguistic diversity. Similarly, the SAGIT's suggestion that rules be developed on how trade disciplines would apply to cultural policy is a sensible proposition that would greatly reduce the uncertainty that presently exists.

For the SAGIT's cultural instrument to work, it will need to have some more meat on its bones. Concrete ideas will have to be developed and strategies refined. For this to succeed, trade negotiators and representatives of the cultural community will have to build a good working relationship. Are the two sides up to it?

WORKING TOWARDS A SOLUTION ON TRADE AND CULTURE

Canadian trade negotiators will be under tremendous pressure to leave culture out of the next round of trade negotiations. Some of this pressure could well come from our own Minister for Canadian Heritage. There is a huge temptation to be protectionist about culture since that is the easiest path to follow.

However, it is in the best interests of our cultural sector to resist this temptation strongly.

The Canadian cultural community faces some immediate concerns. The WTO decision on magazines has left us with much uncertainty about our cultural policy instruments. The American cultural industry can barely restrain its appetite for the balance of our market and is unlikely to be satisfied for long with its resounding win on magazines. Rather than being forced to negotiate market access with the United States on a case-by-case basis, as we did after our loss at the WTO, or travel regularly to defend ourselves in Geneva, we would be well advised to make some sense of the trade policy void that we now occupy.

Our first course of action should be to look critically at the measures we now use to support and promote culture in this country. Many of these policy instruments are already under serious pressure from technological innovation and have lost their usefulness. Others are blatantly inconsistent with our international trade obligations. Instead of vowing to defend our policy tools to the death, why not take the opportunity offered by the upcoming trade negotiations to bring our cultural policy into the twenty-first century?

This would mean less emphasis on ownership restrictions and content requirements, policies that are inadequate in the Internet and satellite age in any event. This will leave subsidies as the instrument of choice for supporting our cultural producers.

Subsidies are not favoured by their recipients in the cultural world who realize that they are easier for the public to observe and for governments to take away than other types of support. Their visibility makes them a bigger target than other more hidden but equally costly and more distorting forms of support. However, subsidies have many endearing qualities. First, they can be more effectively targeted to reward the types of activity that the public considers desirable. Instead of supporting book sellers, broadcasters and song writers just because they are Canadian, as our "Can-Con" and investment restrictions do, subsidy programmes can be designed to encourage the dissemination of Canadian stories, news and ideas. But the most important feature of subsidy programmes is their transparency. This is better from a trade perspective and it makes for better public policy.

In terms of a WTO agenda, negotiators need to focus on several things. First, they should attempt to clarify whether cultural products like films and magazines are bound by the provisions of the GATS or of the GATT agreements. Second, they should craft rules to ensure that certain subsidies to the cultural sector cannot be challenged by a foreign competitor, just as is already the case for R&D, environmental, and regional assistance subsidies,. Third, to ensure that countries do not take undue advantage of special rules for culture, negotiators should define culture and cultural industries as precisely as possible. Above all, negotiators should avoid drafting grandiose statements on the importance of such things as cultural diversity. Such pronouncements amount to little more than deceptive public relations for the folks back home and end up creating a lot of unnecessary confusion in the application of WTO provisions.

Ultimately, Canada's interests are best served by a system that affirms the basic principles of non-discrimination, fairness and transparency. These fundamental principles should guide the conduct of our domestic cultural policy and should govern the treatment of our cultural producers in world markets. The WTO negotiations offer a chance to develop solid rules to allow countries to support legitimate cultural endeavours while reducing the barriers facing cultural exporters. All that is needed is for us to stay focused and remind ourselves what really is at stake. It is not protection for its own sake. Rather, it is about the development and exchange of ideas by and about Canadians. Surely this is something that we have to take an expansive view of.

Chapter 11

Greening the Rules

GLOBAL ENVIRONMENTAL CONCERNS

Seen from space, the Earth is a lovely blue and green sphere enveloped in white, whispy clouds. Back on the ground though, in one of the world's mushrooming mega-cities, the picture is not as pretty. The air is choked with black industrial smoke and the rivers are brown with industrial and residential waste.

Global ecosystems are coming under increasing stress from human activity. The global common is being abused. The overall global environment is becoming more and more fragile. Planet Earth faces problems of global warming, desertification, the destruction of the rainforest, the extinction of species, the loss of bio-diversity, water and air pollution, and the contamination of soils. These are all extremely serious, some would even say to the point of threatening the future of humankind on our planet.

Many environmentalists blame the WTO for doing little to solve environmental problems. This is no doubt true as the WTO is an organization set up to administer the rules of the international trading system and is not the international environmental policing agency. Some environmentalists even take their criticism of the WTO farther and hold it responsible for worsening environmental problems, claiming that it is encouraging "a race to the bottom" with respect to environmental standards. This is an obvious misrepresentation of the facts.

While the WTO's mandate is not to protect the global environment, its impact on the environment still needs to be taken into account. "What has the WTO been doing and what can it do for the environment?" are important questions for everyone, not just for environmentalists.

Economists view environmental problems as arising when all environmental costs of economic activity are not borne by the beneficiaries of the activity –

the so called "negative environmental externalities." In this case, the unfettered functioning of the free market will lead to the production of too much of the good in question. Economists prescribe environmental policies that seek to internalize these externalities and to restore the optimum allocation of resources, including environmental resources of clean air, water and soil.

But even if national governments are successful in establishing environmental policies that successfully internalize all national externalities (and only the most naive economist would ever argue that they are), there are still international externalities to consider. Since these are not borne by national governments or their citizens, there is little reason for national governments to take them into account and in fact none do fully. There are many examples of such externalities. The most global are the so called greenhouse gases – carbon dioxide, nitrous oxide and methane – emitted by the burning of fossil fuels and by agricultural production. Examples of more regional externalities would be untreated sewage in rivers flowing across national boundaries and certain air pollutants such as sulfur dioxide that cause acid rain.

Trade actions are one possible response to cross-border environmental damage. From the point of view of economic theory, however, trade actions are not usually the best response as they introduce production and consumption inefficiencies by distorting the relative prices of domestic and international goods. Better measures usually exist in theory that can produce the same environmental result at a higher level of output and income. But in some cases, trade actions may be the best practical response even if they are not the best response from a theoretical point of view. One example is when the imported goods themselves are the potential source of the damage as in the case of hazardous or nuclear wastes. Another example is where the production techniques used on one side of the border are the cause of the damage on the other such as when untreated wastewater from a food processing plant is dumped in to a river upstream from the border.

Trade measures can also be useful as levers in encouraging lagging countries to introduce policies that are environmentally sound from a global point of view. An example of such a policy where it may be appropriate to consider trade measures in the future is the Kyoto Protocol target for the reduction in greenhouse gas emissions. These gases are believed to be the cause of global warming, which could be a serious threat to life on our planet. The Kyoto Protocol commits signatory countries to reduce these emissions 6 per cent from 1990 levels by 2008-12 Although trade sanctions are not specifically authorized in the Kyoto Protocol, they may ultimately prove necessary if the target is to be met. Since currently only developed countries and Eastern European countries that are signatories of the Protocol have quantitative targets for reductions, it will be necessary to find some means to get developing countries also to reduce greenhouse gases. After all, it wouldn't make much sense to force domestic industries in developed countries to comply with stiff greenhouse gas emission requirements if their offshore competitors in developing countries were not to be subjected to similar requirements. The overall effect of this would be just to encourage greenhouse-gas-intensive economic activity to move offshore and not to reduce greenhouse gases at all. Trade sanctions could prevent this from happening and provide some protection to domestic industries that are forced to comply with the greenhouse gas reduction requirements. They would also encourage developing countries to sign on to the Protocol.

Trade measures have been used successfully to achieve environmental objectives in at least two important instances. Under the Montreal Protocol, there was a ban on the import of CFCs and other substances that were damaging the ozone layer. This encouraged other countries that were not signatories to stop using CFCs too, since they could no longer export products that used CFCs such as refrigerators. The ban was thus successful in ending the use of CFCs and preventing further damage to the ozone layer. Under the Convention on International Trade in Endangered Species (CITES), there was also a trade ban, this time on ivory. It helped to stem the decline in African elephants, which were being slaughtered for their tusks.

THE WTO AGREEMENTS AND THE ENVIRONMENT

The Preamble to the WTO Agreement mentions the objective of sustainable development and the need to protect and preserve the environment. Under WTO rules, countries are allowed to impose trade restrictions for environmental and for health reasons. Two provisions in GATT Article XX permit governments to take measures to protect the environment: section (b) for measures "necessary to protect human, animal or plant life or health"; and section (g) for measures "relating to the conservation of exhaustible natural resources." To qualify, measures cannot involve arbitrary or unjustifiable discrimination or be disguised trade restrictions. An additional, more controversial, qualification set out in Articles I and III proscribes discrimination based on process and production methods (PPM). This means that taxes and regulations on imported goods must be the same as those on domestic regardless of the PPM used in producing the good. This is important because the process and production methods utilized often have significant environmental consequences with some methods generating much more pollution than others.

The Agreement on Technical Barriers to Trade (TBT) and the Sanitary and Phytosanitary Agreement (SPS), which together allow measures for the protection of human, animal and plant life, and health, or the environment, also impose disciplines on technical regulations and SPS measures. Again such regulations and measures can't discriminate between countries or constitute disguised trade barriers. In addition, there is a "necessity test" that requires the regulations or measure to be no more trade restrictive than necessary. SPS measures must also be based on scientific evidence. Furthermore, regulations and measures that are based on international standards are presumed to be consistent with the agreements. SPS measures can be stricter than international norms if there is a scientific justification and if they are supported by an appropriate risk assessment. Finally, regulations and measures must also be transparent if they depart from international standards. Eco-labelling programmes are another important environmental policy instruments that are subject to the disciplines of the Agreement on TBT.

Other WTO Agreements also have environmental provisions. The Agriculture Agreement excludes environmental subsidies from the agricultural subsidy totals that must be cut back. The Agreement on Subsidies and Countervailing Measures makes non-actionable government assistance to industry for up to 20 per cent of the cost of upgrading existing facilities to comply with new environmental legislation. The General Agreement on Trade in Services, similarly to GATT Article XX, permits measures "necessary to protect human, animal or plant life or health" in Article XIV (b). The TRIPs Agreement can facilitate access to environmentally-friendly technology and products. Its Article 27 (2) allows the refusal of patents "to protect human, animal or plant life or health or to avoid serious prejudice to the environment." Article 27 (3) allows the exclusion from patentability of "plants and animals... and essentially biological processes."

Countries are becoming more sensitive about the impact of trade negotiations on the environment. Under pressure from environmental groups, the European Union, the United States and Canada all intend to carry out environmental reviews of the proposals for trade liberalization that come up in the round.

SOME RECENT WTO DECISIONS ENRAGE ENVIRONMENTALISTS

The WTO's bad reputation with environmentalists, particularly in the United States, stems from recent WTO panel decisions on several controversial cases against the United States – the Tuna-Dolphin, the Shrimp-Turtle, and the Gasoline Standards case. In each of these, the rulings limited the ability of the United States to enforce its environmental laws, and have led, or will lead, to a watering down of these laws.

The Tuna-Dolphin case arose from a complaint by Mexico in 1991 under the old GATT regime that its exports of yellowfin tuna to the United States had been banned. The Mexican tuna was embargoed because the Mexican government was unable to prove to the US Authorities that the tuna had been caught using fishing techniques that protected dolphins as required under the US Marine Mammal Protection Act. This Act forbids the sale in the United States of tuna caught using the mile-long nets favoured by Mexico that were notorious for killing the large schools of dolphins that typically swam above the tuna, revealing their location. The embargo on Mexican tuna also applied to intermediary countries, including Canada, that processed and canned Mexican tuna.

The panel ruled that the United States could not ban tuna products from Mexico simply because the way the tuna was caught did not meet US regulations. This decision was based on the GATT Article III proscription against discrimination based on process and production methods. The panel also concluded that the United States could not take trade action to enforce its own domestic laws in other countries such as Mexico in this case. Under the old GATT regime, the United States never had to formally accept the ruling. It was able to maintain its restrictions during lengthy bilateral consultations with Mexico and in the face of another, contrary ruling by a second panel requested by the European Union to enforce the decision of the first. During this time, observers were introduced on Mexican tuna fishing boats and there were some improvements in Mexico's fishing practices but not enough to satisfy environmentalists and the US government. Nevertheless, the United States eventually agreed to comply with the ruling. Amendments to the MMPA proposed by the Clinton Administration will soon allow foreign tuna to be imported even though it is still caught using mile-long nets lethal to dolphins. And to add insult to injury in the view of environmentalists, the tuna will be able to qualify for the label, "dolphin-safe."

The Shrimp-Turtle case was launched in 1997 by India, Malaysia, Pakistan and Thailand against a US ban on the import of shrimp caught using nets without a turtle-excluder device (TED). This is a metal grid sewn into a net which protect turtles by guiding them through a hole in the net. In contrast, shrimp pass through the grid into the back of the net where they are captured. Nets without these devices are the biggest killers of sea turtles, which are listed as endangered species under the CITES. The US Endangered Species Act requires foreign countries selling shrimp in the United States to use nets with TEDs. The WTO panel, supported by the Appellate Body, confirmed the earlier Tuna-

Dolphin decision and ruled that the United States could not ban the import of products that did not meet US PPM regulations. Again the United States was slapped on the wrist for attempting the extraterritorial application of its domestic environmental laws.

The Gasoline Standards case against the United States was the first heard under the new WTO dispute settlement mechanism in 1995-96. Venezuela and Brazil challenged a US Environmental Protection Agency (EPA) rule, which enforced Congressionally-mandated clean air standards to reduce smog and toxic air pollutants, on the grounds that it discriminated against their exports. The standards required that the cleanliness of gasoline sold in the most polluted US cities improve by 15 per cent and that gasoline sold elsewhere in the US maintain 1990 levels. For operational purposes, the EPA rule established a standard for contaminants in gas from domestic and foreign refiners without adequate documentation on their 1990 levels of contaminants, such as those in Venezuela and Brazil, that was based on the 1990 average of all refiners able to provide documentation. The WTO panel ruling, confirmed by the Appellate Body, was that the EPA rules discriminated against foreign refineries. Consequently, the United States relaxed the standards.

In contrast, a 1994 GATT panel ruling on a EU challenge of the US gas guzzler tax and other conservation measures ruled in favour of the United States even though the US exempted primarily US-produced small trucks and utility vehicles from the fleet-wide, fuel-efficiency standards. This exemption made the required reduction in fleet-wide average gasoline consumption much larger for European automobile manufacturers. A clearer case of disguised protectionism is hard to find.

For those interested in the legal fine points, it is worth noting that, while the Shrimp-Turtle and Gasoline Standards cases both ruled against the United States, they provided a different interpretation on the issue of the "extra-jurisdictional" application of domestic laws than in the Dolphin-Tuna case. Based on these cases, it is now accepted that measures "necessary to protect human, animal or plant life or health" Article XX (b) and measures "relating to the conservation of exhaustible natural resources" Article XX (g) can be applied "extra-juridictionally" as long as the measures are really "necessary" and are not a "disguised restriction on international trade." The earlier decision against the United States in the Dolphin-Tuna case is attributed by some trade law experts to the fact that the United States acted unilaterally before taking a reasonable approach to try to resolve the issue and not to any inherent prohibition on the "extra-jurisdictional" application of domestic law.

In another, environmentally-related case, Canada, which produces 95 per cent of exported asbestos, is the complainant against a EU ban on asbestos imports, which applies even to asbestos embedded in building materials. It claims that the ban is a violation of the Technical Barriers to Trade Agreement and runs counter to GATT Articles XI and III banning quantitative restrictions on imports and discriminatory trade measures. The EU counterclaim is based on the right to a safe workplace free of a known carcinogen. However, while there is ample scientific evidence on the carcinogenic properties of asbestos, it is not clear that asbestos in building materials constitutes a threat to human health. A panel decision is awaited.

A final case with environmental implications, which is discussed fully in Chapter 3 above, is the EU ban on beef treated with growth hormones. Suffice it to say here that it puts limits on the extent to which any country can set its own food standards that are higher than international standards unless they are backed by substantial scientific evidence. The precautionary principle, which applies to drugs and requires the manufacturer to demonstrate that a drug is safe, does not apply to foods, which are governed by the less strict criterion of risk assessment.

UNILATERAL VS. MULTILATERAL ACTION

A common element in all the WTO decisions in the cases involving environmental issues is an abhorrence of unilateral trade action. Such actions are considered to be inconsistent with a rules-based international trading system. They allow large industrialized countries like the United States to throw their economic weight around to the disadvantage of smaller, often developing, countries. However, there is little recognition that for environmental problems unilateral action may be the only action possible and that some action is better than none given the gravity of the situation.

The WTO's preferred instruments for dealing with international environmental issues are strengthened multilateral environmental agreements (MEAs). There are about 200 of these instruments, which are usually negotiated under the United Nations Environment Programme. Around 20 of these MEAs have trade bans or rely on trade sanctions for enforcement. The CITES is an example of an agreement that allows the imposition of trade sanctions on countries threatening endangered species. The Kyoto Protocol is an example of a MEA without trade sanctions. So far, no WTO panel has yet been faced with a clear cut case of the use of trade sanctions mandated by an MEA. How such a case would be decided is anyone's guess.

HOW TO GREEN THE WTO

After over twenty years of discussion and debate on trade and the environment in the GATT, the WTO, the OECD and elsewhere, the time has come for action to make the WTO more environmentally-friendly. Surely, it is not beyond our capacity to reach agreement on some ways to make sure the WTO treads more softly in the sensitive environmental field and does not overturn domestic environmental laws unless they are truly discriminatory and constitute disguised barriers to trade.

The WTO Agreements need to be modified to make clear that the essential principles of non-discrimination for environmental measures should be national treatment and most-favoured-nation. GATT Article III also needs to be amended to make clear that prohibitions on restraints on process and production methods do not apply to environmental measures. This is very important because many of the most pressing environmental problems that must be addressed such as reductions in greenhouse gas emissions may have to be handled on the level of process and production methods. Trade-Related Environmental Measures (TREMs) should not be the first weapons in our environmental arsenal, but they should be available for use where necessary.

There are many proposals to make the WTO more environmentally-friendly. Even though the United States has borne the brunt of the WTO challenges of domestic environmental legislation, the European Union has been more progressive than the United States on the environment front and has provided leadership in attempting to green the WTO. At Singapore, the EU proposed that the WTO recognize MEAs that utilize trade sanctions and that changes to GATT Article XX permit the enforcement of MEAs in violation of WTO rules. Surprisingly, the US didn't support this proposal.

GATT Article XX should also be amended to allow countries to take trade measures to protect endangered species or marine mammals. Changes may have to be made elsewhere in the GATT to make sure that this right is not overruled by other provisions. So far, no panel has accepted the legitimacy of a measure permitted as an Article XX derogation if it were otherwise inconsistent with other GATT provisions.

Another proposal is to substitute a "proportionality test" for the "necessity test" in the WTO TBT and SPS Agreements. Under this, it would just be necessary to show that the environmental benefits of the measure were greater than the trade costs. Under the necessity test now in place, the measure must be the least trade restrictive available.

A final proposal is to eliminate all duties and barriers on environmental goods and services. This would make it cheaper to use the latest technologies to clean up or protect the environment. Canada would also benefit as a leading international supplier of such goods and services.

Success in other areas of the Millennium Round could also contribute to the achievement of environmental objectives. The proposed reduction in agricultural subsidies (discussed in Chapter 3 above) would promote more environmentally sound land use and curtail overproduction which not only wastes water, energy and chemicals, but creates pollution as well. Cuts in fisheries subsidies would reduce over-fishing and the depletion of fish stocks. Unfortunately, there is one particularly environmentally damaging form of subsidies that won't get addressed in the round because they don't directly affect trade. These are coal subsidies, which encourage the burning of a particularly dirty fossil fuel.

The WTO's Committee on Trade and Environment (CTE) was created with much fanfare as a result of the Uruguay Round purportedly to make the WTO greener. Environmentalists argue with some justification that, contrary to its initial promise, it has acted perversely identifying environmental measures that need to be eliminated to avoid trade disputes and advancing proposals for greater constraints on the ability to enforce MEAs through trade sanctions. The CTE needs to become greener in its outlook.

Developing countries can be expected to resist the legitimization of TREMs, which they consider a particularly insidious form of disguised protectionism directed largely at them. But the developing countries need to recognize that they are not the worst polluters, and that all of humanity will gain from an improved global environment.

It's the industrial countries of the North that burn the most fossil fuels and produce the most greenhouse gases. This is believed to be the cause of global warming which could have a devastating effect on the global environment if it hasn't started to already. Developing countries, largely in the South, still produce less greenhouse gas than the industrialized countries and are not the main cause of global warming. But in the next century, if developed countries are successful in meeting the Kyoto Protocol targets, the developing countries, which are not signatories of the Protocol, will overtake the developed world as the leading producers of greenhouse gases. It's for this reason that some have argued that the Kyoto Protocol with its coverage limited to industrialized countries was inadequate and would only slow the progress of global warming by twenty years or so.

The Millennium Round offers a unique opportunity for a much larger North-South consensus to improve the global environment. The countries of the North could offer liberalized access to their markets to the countries of the South in return for enforceable commitments to reduce greenhouse gas emissions. In addition, as part of the package, the North could also seek commitments from the South on the conservation of rain forests. They are an important source of the world's oxygen supply by breaking down the carbon dioxide in the air. They are also invaluable reservoirs of global bio-diversity. Furthermore, the package could be sweetened, as suggested by Jeffrey Sachs in a recent article in *The Economist*, by transfers of funds from the North to the South derived from a new proposed carbon tax on Northern fossil fuel consumption. More realistically, this is all probably dreaming in technicolour given the lack of past progress on environmental issues. Countries were all ready to make firm commitments to reduce greenhouse gasses under the Kyoto protocol, but very few have yet ratified it and actual performance has been very disappointing against the benchmark established. Nevertheless, we have to keep trying to make progress on the environment on all fronts, including the WTO.

THE ENVIRONMENTAL BENEFITS OF TRADE LIBERALIZATION

It's also important not to forget the environmental benefits of trade liberalization. The economic growth produced will raise income all around. The increases in income can be used to improve the environment. Richer countries tend to spend a larger portion of their GDP on improving the environment. The technology diffusion facilitated by trade makes the latest and usually more environmentally-friendly technology more widely available. This also will have a positive impact on the environment. Trade liberalization is good for the environment and can be made even better if the rules are greened.

Chapter 12

Integrating Labour Standards

The official position of WTO Members is that labour standards are not on the WTO agenda. But it could be that the lady doth protest too much. The US Administration is pushing hard for something on labour standards to take home from Seattle. Without this something, however symbolic it might be, it will be difficult, if not impossible, for the Administration to garner the necessary additional Democratic Party votes in Congress to pass the fast-track legislation required for the successful conduct and particularly for a successful conclusion of the Millennium Round. The Administration is keen to find some way to quiet "fair-trade" Democrats and their supporters in the AFL-CIO, who have been railing tirelessly against the bogeyman of unfair competition from sweatshops in low-wage countries.

Developing countries, whose prosperity depends on exports of cheap labour-intensive goods to industrialized countries, are equally adamant that nothing be done to undermine their comparative advantage in these goods. For these countries, labour standards are nothing less than a politically correct cloak for protectionism.

The WTO wrestled mightily with these competing views at the 1996 Singapore Ministerial and came up with the following motherhood declaration:

"We renew our commitment to the observance of internationally recognized core labour standards. The International Labour Organization (ILO) is the competent body to set and deal with these standards, and we affirm our support for its work in promoting them. We believe that economic growth and development fostered by increased trade and further trade liberalization contribute to the promotion of these standards. We reject the use of labour standards for protectionist purposes, and agree that the comparative advantage of countries, particularly the low-wage developing countries, must in no way be put into question. In this regard, we note that the WTO and ILO Secretariats will continue their existing collaboration."

CORE LABOUR STANDARDS

Labour standards are the responsibility of the International Labour Organization (ILO). The ILO is a UN-affiliated body made up of representatives of governments, workers, and employers from 174 member countries. Since 1919, the ILO's annual Conferences have passed heaps of conventions on labour standards. Seven of these conventions constitute what the ILO calls "core labour standards:"

- Convention number 87 on freedom of association;
- Convention number 98 on collective bargaining;
- Conventions number 29 and 105 on freedom from forced labour;
- Convention number 100 on equal remuneration;
- Convention number 111 on non-discrimination in employment; and
- Convention number 138 on the minimum working age.

These so-called "enabling rights" do not cover wages or working conditions. Rather, they provide the framework within which wages and working conditions are determined. The trade unions that are well represented at the ILO are naturally enough big supporters of the right to freedom of association and collective bargaining. In this, they differ from some economists who believe that union monopolies distort resource allocation just like business monopolies and should be similarly outlawed.

For years, the ILO was content to sit around in Geneva with stacks of its labour standard conventions that had yet to be ratified by all of its members. Only 35 members have ratified all seven of the core conventions. One of the worst footdraggers among its members was the current champion of labour standards, the United States, which had only ratified the convention on the abolition of forced labour. The problem was that unless a convention was passed by its members, the ILO had no mandate to monitor its application and enforcement.

With the debate on labour standards raging all about it, the ILO finally had to do something. At the ILO Conference in June 1998, a declaration was ratified by the ILO members specifying that:

"all members, even if they have not ratified the Conventions in question, have an obligation arising from the very fact of membership in the Organization, to respect, to promote and to realize, in good faith and in accordance with the Constitution, the principles concerning the fundamental rights which are the subject of the Conventions, namely:

(a) freedom of association and the effective recognition of the right of collective bargaining;

(b) the elimination of all forms of forced or compulsory labour;

(c) the effective abolition of child labour;

(d) the elimination of discrimination in respect of employment and occupation."

With this new declaration, countries will be required to report annually on the progress they have made in meeting these four fundamental rights. The ILO will in turn issue an annual report on global progress. Hopefully, this report will be hard hitting and pull no punches. International public opinion can be a powerful force for improvement once the spotlight is turned on particular abuses of labour rights.

In the same June 1998 declaration, ILO members "stressed that labour standards should not be used for protectionist purposes, and that nothing in this declaration and its follow-up shall be invoked or otherwise used for such purposes; in addition, the comparative advantage of any country should be in no way called into question by this declaration and its followup." That the language is almost the same as used in the WTO Singapore Ministerial declaration is no coincidence. They were singing from the same hymnal. It is not only at the WTO that countries express their reservations about making links between labour standards to trade sanctions. Jawboning seems to be the preferred alternative.

Child labour is a particularly contentious issue. While everyone abhors the exploitation of children, there is genuine concern that efforts to prevent poor children from working could end up making them and their families even worse off. Some forms of child labour, though, are so abhorrent to everyone that it was possible to reach agreement to adopt a convention banning the worst forms of child labour at this year's annual ILO conference. The convention, which applies to all persons under 18, calls for measures to stop: "all forms of slavery or practices similar to slavery, such as the sale and trafficking of children, debt bondage, serfdom and forced or compulsory labour; forced or compulsory recruitment of children for use in armed conflict; use of a child for prostitution, production of pornography or pornographic performances; use, procuring or offering of a child for illicit activities, in particular for the production and the trafficking of drugs; and, work which is likely to harm the health, safety or morals of children." In deference to the views of developing countries, there is no outright prohibition on work by very young children such as exists in almost all industrialized countries.

Cartoon by Clay Bennett, *The Christian Science Monitor.* Reprinted with his permission.

WHY THE WTO?

The WTO is not close to the hearts of most trade unionists. Many view it as an uppity institution, usurping national sovereignty and forcing reluctant governments to yield to global market forces. Yet at the same time, they do give it a grudging respect, which they may not have for their own handmaiden, the more passive ILO. Trade unionists see the WTO protecting business from unfair competition and ask why it can't do the same for them. In their view, the threat of trade sanctions that the WTO has at its disposal is a powerful tool that can be wielded for good as well as evil. The ILO may be able to bark, but the WTO can bite. This is just what trade unionists feel is needed to make rapid progress on labour standards after too many years of inaction. The trick is to get the WTO to put its teeth at the service of labour standards in a politically-acceptable and non-trade-distorting manner.

WHAT, IF ANYTHING, IS THE WTO DOING ALREADY?

In a nutshell, not much. Article XX (e) of the GATT 1947 permits WTO Members to take measures against "the products of prison labour." Reference to slave labour, child labour or any other type of forced labour is conspicuously absent. Under the WTO agreements, a country could prohibit the import of products produced by prisoners, but could do absolutely nothing about goods made by slaves, not that there are probably very many still around producing internationally traded goods.

THE NAFTA APPROACH

The North American Agreement on Labor Cooperation (NAALC), which was tagged on to the NAFTA at the last minute, was a response to the fearsome prospect of Ross Perot's "giant sucking sound." While it does not establish common minimum standards, it commits the NAFTA partners to promote the following guiding principles:

- freedom of association and the right to organize;
- the right to bargain collectively;
- the right to strike;
- prohibition of forced labour;
- labour protection for children and young persons;
- minimum employment standards;
- elimination of employment discrimination;
- equal pay for women and men;
- prevention of occupational injuries and illnesses;
- compensation in cases of occupational injuries and illnesses; and
- protection of migrant workers.

These labour principles go far beyond the ILO's core labour standards. In addition, an institutional framework was established to oversee the Agreement which includes a Commission for Labor Cooperation with a Secretariat in Dallas, Texas, and National Administrative Offices in each of the NAFTA countries. A dispute settlement mechanism was also created with consultation and arbitral panels.

The most common complaints under the Agreement have been filed by US unions against Mexican companies that have allegedly violated the right of unions to organize. A complaint was also launched by a coalition of Mexican unions and supported by American unions accusing the Washington state apple industry of violating the rights of Mexican apple pickers and threatening their health and safety.

The achievements of the NAALC may not be very impressive to trade unionists. But even they must admit that the agreement represents a pioneering effort to introduce labour standards into a trade agreement. It might eventually serve as a model for a multilateral agreement under the WTO. However, the world is not yet ready to contemplate such an ambitious solution to the labour standards issue.

WHAT CAN BE DONE?

One of the most controversial proposals is to add a "social clause" in the WTO agreements that would allow trade sanctions to be used to enforce core labour standards. Under this proposal, the ILO would be responsible for monitoring compliance and identifying violations while the WTO would determine and administer the appropriate trade remedies. This would be a departure from the usual practice as the WTO does not administer multilateral sanctions, but authorizes compensating trade measures to restore previously negotiated trade benefits. Judging from the statements on using labour standards for protectionist purposes contained in both the WTO Singapore Ministerial Declaration and the ILO Declaration on fundamental principles and rights of work, there is little enthusiasm for this proposal at either the WTO or the ILO.

Another possibility would be to add a provision for products of forced labour similar to that for prison labour contained in Article XX of GATT 1947. Forced labour runs contrary to the fundamental principle of voluntary exchange which underlies market-based economies. Even though this proposal would not be a major change, it still could run into opposition from some developing countries.

Even more controversial would be the addition of a provision to Article XX for the products of children under, say, 12. But even from a narrow economic point of view, let alone the social, it's not in the interest of any developing country to allow children to work rather than to complete their primary education. And the labour of very young children is not voluntary and is usually forced by their parents constituting nothing more than a particular type of forced labour. Nevertheless, any restrictions on child labour would be strongly resisted by many developing countries.

The EU has an incentive scheme that provides extra benefits to developing countries that are eligible for lower GSP tariffs if they can demonstrate that they meet core labour standards. Other developed countries could also consider providing such a carrot. The EU, which opposes any efforts to use labour standards for protectionist purposes, advocates the use of such positive measures rather than the stick of trade sanctions. The EU is considering a proposal to establish some kind of forum to oversee labour standards. This forum could be inside the WTO, joint between the WTO and ILO, or outside the WTO entirely.

Through its Trade Policy Review Mechanism, the WTO could also be involved in monitoring labour standards, particularly in Export Processing Zones (EPZs), which are directly related to trade. As part of a package of tax and other incentives, some countries have offered waivers from national labour laws, especially those relating to union rights, to foreign companies setting up in the EPZ. Other countries just don't enforce their labour standards in EPZs. In these limited cases, a direct link can be established between trade and lower labour standards.

The WTO and the ILO will definitely need to work together more closely to ensure that core labour standards are respected, and that, more generally, progress is made in improving standards of living and working conditions.

Nothing substantive may get done on labour standards in the Millennium Round. But there will at least be something symbolic. More substance will probably have to await future rounds. At least a start can be made now.

Freer trade will increase productivity and incomes. This may be the most important contribution of a successful Millenium Round to labour standards. As a rule, the countries with the highest incomes also have the highest labour standards. Labour standards, and not only cash standards, will improve with incomes. Some of the least developed countries still have the dismal labour standards that Dickens chronicled for England during the Industrial Revolution, largely because they have similarly low levels of income. Economic development and improved labour standards go together.

Chapter 13

Settling Disputes

THE WTO'S CROWNING GLORY

The WTO's dispute settlement system is perhaps the greatest single accomplishment of the Uruguay Round of trade negotiations. So much so that everyone from human rights advocates to environmentalists want access to it. They recognize that the WTO's mechanism for resolving disputes is truly unique among international institutions in that it actually has some teeth.

While the dispute settlement mechanism works well, there are a couple of areas that need improvement in the next round of trade negotiations.

SINGING ITS PRAISES

The WTO's settlement procedures are a vast improvement over the previous system that existed under the GATT. Under the old GATT regime, countries could ignore the decisions of panels with impunity. Even Canada, the boy scouts that we are, did so on occasion. The result was that countries felt it was hardly worth pursuing a trade dispute since, even if they won, there was no guarantee that anything would change in the end.

The new system makes panel and Appellate Body decisions binding. Countries whose practices are found to be inconsistent with WTO obligations must bring their measures into conformity or face the prospect of WTO-sanctioned countermeasures.

The WTO panel decisions can be appealed, something that was not possible under the previous GATT system. The WTO Appellate Body (AB) is a permanent group of seven individuals, each appointed for a term of up to eight years. While the AB considers only matters of law and does not rehear the facts of a case, the possibility of an appeal was important in getting members to agree to be bound by dispute settlement decisions.

Countries that get embroiled in disagreements are required to consult for at least 60 days in an effort to reach a mutually satisfactory "out of court" resolution. If consultations are unsuccessful, the dispute proceeds through a series of steps from the creation of a dispute settlement panel, panel hearings, interim and final panel reports, and Appellate Body hearings and report. Despite all these stages, the WTO system has still shaved months off the time the GATT used to take to deal with disputes.

The WTO's Dispute Settlement Understanding provides a single forum for resolving disputes that arise under a handful of WTO agreements, including the GATT, GATS, TRIPs and even some plurilateral agreements like the Agreement on Government Procurement. The single window aspect adds vastly to the coherence and effectiveness of the WTO system.

The Dispute Settlement Body has been instrumental in convincing the developing world of the utility of the WTO. The very first case brought was a developing country's challenge of a developed country practice – Venezuela and Brazil's case against the US on gasoline. The fact that newer Members of the WTO are guaranteed access to and have made ample use of the dispute settlement provisions has been central in dispelling the notion that the WTO is an old boys' club.

To the cynics, the huge proliferation of WTO disputes suggests that the system is out of control and that judicial policy is trying to take over trade policy. In fact, it demonstrates something quite different. The effectiveness of the dispute settlement procedures shows the faith that WTO Members have placed in the agreements they negotiated. Their willingness to use the system shows their commitment to a rules-based system for liberalizing world trade.

THE RESULTS

The best evidence of the superiority of the new system is the use that it gets. In the 47 years of the GATT, some 300 disputes were brought for resolution, an average of 6 or 7 per year. By late September 1999, less than six years into its operation, the WTO's Dispute Settlement Body had received 180 requests for consultation representing 140 separate cases. This is over five times the annual caseload handled under the GATT.

By our tally, there have been 140 separate WTO disputes (Table 2). As cases often involve multiple parties and can disappear only to reappear later, totals under each category are approximate estimates. The difficulties of precision aside, however, two striking facts stand out in the table. The first is that many disputes are resolved during the consultation stage and are then settled or withdrawn. The importance of consultation is even more apparent when one recognizes that a large number of cases have languished in consultation for some time. The second observation is that almost all cases that proceed to the stage of a panel report end up going on to appeal.

STRETCHED RESOURCES

The success of the dispute settlement mechanism has put severe strains on the system. It is being used to the point of being over burdened.

The requirement to create qualified panels within the short time frame stipulated in the WTO provisions has proven to be a difficult challenge. The panels are made up from a list of candidates put forward by WTO Member countries. Ideally, panel members have a knowledge of international trade and are either lawyers or trade specialists who have been active in the field.

Table 2 Use of the WTO Dispute Settlement Mechanism	
Consultation Requests	181
Panel rulings	24
Appellate Body reports	21
Cases withdrawn or settled	37
Pending consultations	66
Total Distinct Cases	140

Source: http://www.wto.org.dispute/bulletin.htm
Compiled September 24, 1999
Note: The figures presented in this table do not add. This is owing to the fact that many of the cases have multiple parties or can be recorded at more than one stage of resolution. For example, a case might have been designated as completed since it is the subject of a panel and Appellate Body ruling. However, one of the challenging parties might request consultations on the same product but under a related but different matter. Alternatively, a Member might reach a negotiated settlement with one of the challenging parties but not the others.

Grumblings are being heard about the quality of some recent WTO panels. Some have come close to unseemly conflict of interest situations. None of this is surprising given the shear number of panels that have been needed in the past five years, the complexity of the issues and the limited number of qualified but independent individuals available with expertise in this specialized area.

Over time, this situation is certain to improve. In the meantime, the growing pains are evident.

One solution might be to create a permanent body of experts who would do nothing but serve on dispute settlement panels. This would make the panel process rather like the WTO Appellate Body, which is a permanent group. While a permanent body would improve the consistency of panel decisions, we would lose the varied perspective and expertise that ad hoc panels bring. Besides, one wonders if we really need another body of Geneva-dwellers that have been captured by the Lac Léman mind-set.

At a minimum, there is a need to expand the number of individuals on the panel roster list and to enlarge the legal, translation and other resource staff. This will be no mean feat since WTO budgetary resources have been flat due to the unwillingness of important contributors to open their pocketbooks wider.

The other burden imposed by the new system is on the resources of the member countries. Even keeping a watching brief on cases before the dispute settlement body, let alone participating as a principal or observer, can prove to be extremely taxing. If developed countries like Canada are feeling the pinch, it is difficult to imagine how countries in the developing world can cope. In fact, many cannot. A case in point is the inability of important Central American banana producers to participate in the recent bananas dispute despite its overwhelming importance to their economies.

While the enthusiasm for dispute settlement might well abate in time, the present strains are proving hard to bear. WTO decisions are having quite fundamental effects on domestic policy making. Moreover, the repercussions of the WTO rulings have extended beyond the countries directly involved in the disputes. To maintain the confidence of Members in the overall system, panels need to have the resources and credentials necessary to do a good job. The Millennium Round provides an opportunity to do something about this. A good start would be to make provision for more generous funding.

Negotiators at the Millennium Round might also give some thought to a programme to assist developing countries to participate more fully in dispute proceedings. The issue is a transitional one since trade expertise in much of the developing world will certainly increase with time. At present, however, the complexity, volume and expense of cases is overwhelming. The interests and perspective of the developing country Members needs to be heard. Otherwise, much of the WTO's effectiveness will be lost. It will come to be perceived, perhaps justifiably, as a club where only rich countries get a chance to a fair hearing.

Improving Compliance

A couple of recent WTO cases have revealed a rather disturbing weakness in the dispute settlement provisions. Getting the losing party to implement a panel report or Appellate Body determination can be a long and messy business.

Dispute Settlement Body determinations are supposed to be binding. If a party's measures are found to be inconsistent with its WTO obligations, the Member must bring its practices into compliance. If they do not, the successful challenger is entitled to take countermeasures of equivalent commercial effect. The countermeasures must be blessed by the WTO and usually take the form of suspending trade concessions or some kind of financial compensation.

While this sounds all very straightforward, it can be anything but in practice. Certain provisions of the Dispute Settlement Understanding, specifically Articles 21.5, 22 and 23, which deal respectively with disagreements over compliance measures, retaliation in cases of non-compliance and discouraging unilateral action, are ambiguous. As a result, it is unclear as to which provision applies in a situation when a challenging Member is unsatisfied with the actions, or inaction, of another Member in response to a WTO panel ruling.

In a couple of recent cases, losing parties have made minor changes to their policies, maintaining that they have complied with WTO requirements. The challenging countries have disagreed, claiming that one non-conforming measure has merely been substituted for another. Because the provisions are unclear, a Member intent on dodging an unfavourable ruling could force its adversaries into a never-ending series of panels, indefinitely delaying implementation of the original ruling.

Compliance became an issue in the American challenge of Europe's banana import regime. After being ruled against in the bananas case, the EU showed no desire to make meaningful changes to its practices. The Americans did not take this news calmly. Not content to wait for guidance on countermeasures from the Dispute Settlement Body, the US threatened to impose a host of trade sanctions of its own. The prospect of unilateral action by any Member, particularly a powerful country like the US, is very damaging for the multilateral trading system whose integrity depends on the coordinated action of all WTO participants. If trading partners as large as the European Union and the United States they are unable to resolve their disputes amicably, what kind of example does this set for newer and less powerful Members of the WTO?

MORE TRANSPARENCY

In crafting the WTO's dispute settlement provisions, negotiators bent over backwards to devise a system that is non-confrontational. Among other things, this meant limiting the hearings and other formal proceedings to official delegates representing the countries involved in the dispute. It also meant restricting the circulation of documents to only the parties involved in the dispute.

The desire was well-intended. A low-key, conciliatory approach is more likely to result in negotiated compromises than a winner-takes-all litigious model. The idea was that if one could keep the private trade lawyers out, especially the $400-per-hour, Gucci-loafer-wearing, Washington D.C. variety of trade lawyer, we would all be a lot better off.

The trouble is that all the secrecy that surrounds the proceedings gives off a bad aura. A lot of important things are being decided by WTO panels. Panel and Appellate Body reports can significantly change the way that governments conduct their business. This is even for countries that were not involved in the disputes under consideration. It is only appropriate that non-member participants be given an opportunity to attend the proceedings and read the submissions filed.

Those opposed to the idea of more transparency raise concerns that confidential information will be released. Unless Members are confident that proper safeguards are in place, they will not come forward with the information panels require to do their work.

The protection of truly confidential information can still be accomplished in a more open and transparent system. Canada has already taken a step in this direction by pledging to prepare non-confidential summaries of any submissions it makes to the WTO. While it has to tighten up its timing to ensure that the public version is available at the same time as the confidential brief is filed in Geneva, and before the juicy bits have already been leaked to the business press, Canada's idea is a good one. Countries involved in disputes should have to file both confidential and non-confidential submissions. The public versions should be immediately available on the WTO website.

This idea would make things a lot easier for the WTO itself. The existing system creates all sorts of confusion and extra work. Some information is in the public domain, while other is not even though there is no real rationale for keeping it secret. WTO panels, who have to prepare public reports, have to go through the considerable effort of paraphrasing information that could otherwise have been taken directly from parties' submissions. The result is that a lot of energy gets expended handling material that really does not need to be protected. Not only does this cost more in the end, but the illusion of secrecy does not engender confidence in the system.

The other argument against more transparency is that WTO panel and Appellate Body proceedings would turn into circuses for the disaffected. Imagine the horror going through the minds of trade bureaucrats at the thought that their sedate existence in Geneva might be disrupted by environmentalists and activists of other ilk. Its enough to make them want to put in for a transfer to the OECD.

There might be good reason to deny non-governmental organizations and others not party to a dispute the right to actually participate in the proceedings. The GATT/WTO tradition has long been one of government-to-government dealings as a way of minimizing rancour and encouraging constructive diplomacy. This does not mean, however, that non-participants should be shut out completely. In addition to being granted access to public briefs and information, they should be allowed to attend panel and Appellate Body proceedings provided confidential information is not being discussed. Although political cultures and structures differ amongst WTO Member governments, they should consider instituting mechanisms for gathering the views of domestic groups, the so-called "civil society". What is more, governments should make sincere attempts to reflect these opinions in their own submissions before dispute settlement bodies.

Finally, there is the issue of interim reports. In the old GATT days, first drafts of panel reports were released on a confidential basis to the countries involved in the case prior to being circulated to all Members. The idea was that the early release would provide those directly affected with an opportunity to catch and correct any mistakes made by the panel. This practice has been carried over to the WTO, even though the job of the Appellate Body makes it redundant. After all, appellate review is supposed to clear up any errors made by the panel.

The interim report business has created no end of confusion. Some governments have not considered themselves bound by the report's confidential status and have commented publicly on its contents. This puts other parties to the dispute in an awkward situation, not wanting to break WTO protocol but being frustrated at being put at a disadvantage in the public relations game. One common scenario is for one party to claim victory in a case upon release of the interim report. Given the complexity of these cases, it is not difficult to find at least one minor point that a panel will decide in a party's favour. The adversary, who might well have been victorious overall, has little recourse. The interim decision is not available for members of the press to analyze for themselves. By the time the official report is released some weeks later, the press and public have lost interest. In the meantime, the folks back home are livid at their trade policy officials for having lost a case that they might really have won.

It is high time to end this messy state of affairs. WTO panel decisions should be released in public and only once. This would place all WTO Members on an equal footing and provide the transparency and openness the public deserves.

The chances are good that reforms will be made to improve the transparency of the dispute settlement system. In its July 29th position paper by WTO Ambassador Esserman, the United States proposed "providing for earlier circulation of panel reports, making parties' submissions to panels public, allowing for submissions of amicus briefs and opening hearings to observers from the public". These proposals were reportedly submitted to the Dispute Settlement Review which is supposed to report and make recommendations to the Seattle Ministerial for ratification. If we are lucky, this might be one of the early-harvest accomplishments in Seattle.

LITTLE DISPUTE OVER DISPUTES

By and large, the WTO's dispute settlement provisions operate remarkably well. The few problems that exist can be solved with increased resources and clearer drafting to remove some ambiguities related to enforcement and compliance. This should be easy to achieve in the Millennium Round negotiations.

The issue of transparency is a tremendously important one. It is crucial to have domestic constituencies on side if we are to advance the cause of trade liberalization. Disputes are dealing with issues that hit very close to the bone in terms of national sovereignty – matters relating to environment, health and safety, for example. The fears of citizens that dispute settlement bodies are over stepping their boundaries and trampling on legitimate national prerogatives need to be addressed and allayed. An important element of that is to remove the intrigue and secrecy that now exists, and make the whole process more open. There is no reason why the non-participating governments and the public at large should not be given more access to dispute proceedings. In fact, the integrity of the system might well depend on it.

Chapter 14

Joining the Club

THE NEED FOR NEW MEMBERS

With the growth in international trade and investment and the spread in market-based strategies for economic development, it is becoming increasingly important that the WTO rules-based international trading system be extended to cover all the world's economies. It is especially important that the larger economies of China and Russia be brought into the WTO club. Countries that are not members of the WTO tend to have much higher tariffs than Members, as well as more barriers to trade.

The benefits of an expanded WTO will accrue to all Members, new as well as old. The newly-acceding countries will benefit from more secure access to the domestic markets of member countries on a most-favored-nation basis. This is vital for their continued growth and prosperity. In return, they will have to open up their domestic markets to exports from WTO Members and subject their economic policies to the disciplines of the WTO agreements, which of and by itself will have very beneficial effects on their economies. The existing WTO Members will also benefit from improved access to the domestic markets of the acceding countries. Any disputes that arise with newly acceding countries will have to be settled under the WTO dispute settlement mechanism rather than by unilateral action. This will help to prevent the resort to beggar-thy-neighbor policies and trade wars.

Bringing China and Russia into the WTO and integrating their economies more closely into the global economy will also improve prospects for world peace. Countries that are dependent on each other to maintain their standards of living don't usually go to war. This was one of the main reasons that France and Germany joined together after the devastation of the Second World War to form the European Coal and Steel Community and later the European Economic Community. Robert Schuman and Jean Monnet, the co-fathers of the

EU, were driven by a vision of an integrated and peaceful Europe that would never again be ravished by war as it had already been twice in the Twentieth Century.

The Accession Process

Under Article XII:1 of the Marrakesh Agreement establishing the WTO, any state (or customs territory possessing full autonomy in the conduct of its external commercial relations and of other matters provided for in the WTO agreements) wishing to join the WTO and accede to the WTO agreements can apply for membership by communicating its desire to the Director-General. The General Council then considers the application and establishes a Working Party to examine it further and to prepare recommendations including a draft Protocol of Accession.

The Working Party begins its investigations by considering a memorandum provided by the applicant that describes its trade regime and tariff schedules in detail. The applicant then is required to defend before the Working Party the conformity of its regime with all the WTO agreements. Once this fact-finding is sufficiently advanced, bilateral negotiations commence either with the applicant tabling its initial offer on goods and services or with interested Members presenting their requests for concessions.

The negotiated terms of accession include acceptance of all the WTO agreements as well as the consolidated results of bilateral negotiations with current WTO Members on schedules of concessions in goods and specific commitments in services. All WTO Members benefit from the bilateral negotiations because they are extended to all Members on a most-favoured-nation basis. The bilateral negotiations with the largest WTO Members, namely the United States, the European Union, and Japan, are obviously the most important as these countries have a de facto veto on new Members. Put another way, they can blackball new members in the club.

A decision on an accession is usually taken by the WTO's General Council after it receives the Draft Report, the Draft Protocol and Schedules on Goods and Services from the Working Party. But according to Article XII:2 of the Marrakesh Agreement, the final decision is the prerogative of the Ministerial Conference like the one held at Seattle. Formally, the terms of accession must be approved by a two-thirds majority of the WTO Members, but by custom a consensus is required. Following this approval, the Protocol of Accession enters into force. The applicant becomes a WTO Member thirty days after it completes its own legal formalities for acceptance.

COUNTRIES NEGOTIATING ACCESSION

WTO/GATT membership has increased sharply since the fall of communism and the completion of the Uruguay Round. Everyone wants to join the WTO, which sets the rules for the global marketplace. The number of members is now 135 up from around 100 in 1990. More recently, there has been some further progress in extending WTO membership. The Kyrgyz Republic and Latvia have just joined and Estonia will officially become a Member on November 13. A further 29 countries and customs territories have applied to join. China, Chinese Taipei (Taiwan), Russia, Saudi Arabia, Ukraine, Lithuania, and Vietnam are among 20 applicants with which active negotiations are proceeding. Seventeen of the countries negotiating accession are transition economies.

Countries Negotiating Accession to the WTO			
Albania	Croatia	Moldova	Sudan
Algeria	FYR Macedonia	Nepal	Chinese Taipei
Andorra	Georgia	Oman	Tonga
Armenia	Jordan	Russian Federation	Ukraine
Azerbaijan	Kazakstan	Samoa	Uzbekistan
Belarus	Laos	Saudi Arabia	Vanuata
Cambodia	Lithuania	Seychelles	Vietnam
China			

Charlene Barshefsky, the US Trade Representative, told the US Senate Agricultural Committee in June that the United States has completed its bilateral negotiations with Chinese Taipei, and has made significant progress with nine other countries including Albania, Armenia, China, Croatia, Georgia, Jordan, Lithuania, Moldova, and Oman. This provides a good indication of the countries that are next in line for accession.

Given the number of countries seeking accession, critics that argue that the WTO is an obstacle to economic development should ask themselves, "Why do so many developing countries want to join?"

CHINA

By far the most important accession negotiations have been those underway for thirteen years with China, a country that exported US$184 million in 1998 and is one of the world's top five traders. The international trading system can hardly be considered global as long as China with its 1.3 billion people or over one-fifth of the world's population remains outside the WTO.

The bilateral negotiations between the United States and China have been very prolonged and difficult. This stemmed from the fundamental philosophical differences that were played out at the negotiating table. The United States wanted China to introduce the stringent liberalization measures imposed on developed countries in the WTO. China felt that it should be allowed to adopt the more lenient measures allowed developing nations.

The seemingly never-ending bilateral negotiations between China and the United States and other countries over accession seemed to be finally nearing an end when Premier Zhu Rongji visited the United States last April. China offered a very attractive package containing concessions on agriculture, including improved access for citrus, wheat and beef, and tariff cuts of more than a half. Non-tariff barriers on a range of agricultural products were to be replaced by tariff rate quotas, which were substantially above current import volumes. Foreigners were to be allowed to own 49 per cent of telecommunication ventures. Tariffs on automobiles were to be cut from 80 per cent to 25 per cent. At that time, the remaining sticking points included US demands for more opening of financial services and telecommunications and US insistence on additional protection for its steel, textiles and clothing industries.

With the benefit of hindsight, it appears that this deal offered by the Chinese Premier may have been the best China was prepared to offer and that some of its elements may no longer be on the table. The Chinese Premier and other Chinese negotiators lost much face when they had to return home from the United States empty handed. This strengthened the hands of those who oppose the economic liberalization required to join the WTO. In contrast, in the United States, business groups criticized the Administration for walking away from what looked to them like a pretty good deal.

If the Chinese Premier's failure to reach agreement after going out on a limb wasn't bad enough, China's prospects of joining the WTO suffered another major setback. Shortly after the Premier returned home, NATO accidently bombed the Chinese Embassy in Belgrade on May 7 precipitating a wave of anti-American demonstrations, including some that vandalized the US Embassy and consulates in China. Meanwhile in the United States, the release of the Congressional report on Chinese nuclear espionage didn't do much to help assuage Congressional opposition to a trade deal with China. Nevertheless, in July the House approved a bill extending normal trade relationships with China for another year.

By early September, the situation had cooled enough for substantive talks to resume. President Bill Clinton and President Jiang Zemin met at the APEC Summit in Auckland on September 10-12. Further talks were held in Washington in late September. The United States was seeking the same deal that had been offered in April plus restrictions on textile exports. China claimed that there were ten or fifteen errors in the reported offer and was seeking "clarifications." Even if the Chinese manage to reach an agreement with the United States soon, there are other hurdles to clear. Bilateral negotiations with other WTO Members including the EU and Canada must be completed. All of this will, of course, take time. Consequently, it now looks increasingly unlikely that China will be admitted into the WTO before the Seattle Ministerial begins in late November. This is unfortunate, as it is desirable that China be a full participant in the next round of multilateral trade negotiations.

Bringing China fully into WTO presents some unique challenges. Much of China's economy is run by state-owned enterprises (SOEs) whose purchasing decisions can be subject to political pressure. This is the reason the United States wants China to sign the Agreement on Government Procurement. In addition, the Chinese government regulation of the financial sector and telecommunications and other sectors tend to favour SOEs. Finally, much of China's trade is conducted by State Trading Enterprises (STE).

It will be impossible to resolve all the outstanding issues prior to China's accession. That will take several rounds of trade negotiations. This is why it is important to bring China into the WTO before the Millennium Round gets well underway. It will subject China to the disciplines of another round of negotiations.

RUSSIA

Russia is the next most important country that is not a Member of the WTO. Negotiations over accession have been underway since 1993. While some progress has been made, the process was slowed by the Russian financial crisis in August 1998 when Russia defaulted on its debt and the ruble collapsed. However, a goods and market access offer and a service offer have recently been circulated. It is important to bring this process to a reasonably swift conclusion. But unfortunately the signs point otherwise. Michael Moore, the new Director General of the WTO who began his three year term in September, offered his assessment that "Russia won't be in my time."

The state-owned sector in Russia has been reduced by privatization, and is no longer as important as it is in China. Nevertheless, there is still a crying need to subject the Russian economy to the disciplines of the WTO agreements. This will provide some protection for Russia's trading partners against the widespread corruption in Russian business and politics that makes trading with Russia so difficult. It should also have some beneficial spillover effects in terms of creating a badly-needed rules-based framework for domestic economic activity.

CANADA'S ROLE

Because of the size of the markets concerned and the extent of the barriers to trade at issue, the accession negotiations are very important for Canada. The Canadian Government, representing Canadian interests, has been an active participant in the WTO Working Parties set up to examine the new applicants trade regime and to identify required reforms. The Canadian Government is also pursuing Canadian interests through bilateral market access negotiations, including most importantly with China and Russia.

Chapter 15

Looking Ahead

THE MILLENNIUM ROUND GETS UNDERWAY

After the end of Seattle's four-day stint as the protest capital of the universe, it will be back to business as usual and the WTO Millennium Round will be officially underway. The Seattle Ministerial Declaration, which was already circulating in draft form in Geneva in September, will set the parameters of the talks. In addition to the WTO committees, which will still continue to function in support of the talks, negotiating structures will be created. Negotiating committees will be set up to deal with the main issues. Working parties will be established to grapple with more technical questions. Bilateral negotiations will be scheduled. And all will be governed by ambitious timetables with tight deadlines. There will be little time to waste arguing about the size and shape of the table.

Concerning the structure of the negotiations, there are two possibilities. One would be to create a separate Trade Negotiations Committee to run the negotiations. Another would be to leave the negotiations under the General Council. The Uruguay Round negotiations was headed up by a separate Trade Negotiations Committee. But at that time there was no WTO and no permanent organizational structure existed. Now that the General Council exists, it would be the logical choice to coordinate the negotiations and the committee structure reporting to it could continue to function as negotiating committees. An advantage of this would be that it would avoid duplication and economize on scarce technical and negotiating expertise both from the member countries and the WTO itself. Many, particularly developing countries, have difficulties fully participating in existing committees and would not be able to participate in a parallel committee structure.

A key milestone in the Millennium Round will be the Fourth Ministerial Meeting, which should take place late in the year 2001. This meeting will probably serve as a mid-term review of the progress of the round like the Montreal Ministerial Meeting in December 1988 did for the Uruguay Round. It will provide an opportunity to take stock, review draft changes to agreements, and identify contentious outstanding issues that need to be resolved before the round can be brought to a successful conclusion.

The Millennium Round negotiations will have the largest number of participants ever. And many of the new participants will be transitional or developing countries that export resources and labour-intensive goods and have much different concerns than the industrialized countries. This will make for a much more complex negotiations and a more volatile negotiating dynamics. In addition, the overall economic climate will be very important for the success of the negotiations. There are huge external imbalances, including most notably a US trade deficit of $250 billion, which have been allowed to build up to unsustainable levels to promote recovery from the Asian crisis. The need to reduce these imbalances will be a continuing source of friction as the round progresses. Second, the US economy is operating at a very high level of activity and low rate of unemployment. Any increase in inflation could trigger a monetary policy response that would have a major impact on the international economy and dramatically affect the climate of negotiations and the prospects for a successful Millennium Round. On the other hand, the issues are easier this time than in the Uruguay Round. The WTO already exists and doesn't need to be created out of nothing. Most of the difficult areas outside the GATT were already brought into the rules-based trading system.

THE NEGOTIATING AGENDA

The Quad countries, particularly the United States and the European Union and to a lesser extent Japan, will as usual be in the driving seat for the Millennium Round. Canada will be going along for the ride, but maybe able to do some selective back seat driving. Other countries, especially the developing countries, will be even further away from the steering wheel, and less likely to influence the direction of the vehicle. But to get a final agreement it will be necessary to find something that is acceptable to the most important of them as well as to the United States, the European Union and Japan. To facilitate this, it might be necessary to create something for the Millennium Round like the G-20, which was formed to deal with international financial issues and includes key developing countries such as India and Brazil.

The big issues are already on the table in the position papers prepared by the main players. Their positions on these issues are summarized in Table 3.

The APEC Leaders meeting in Auckland in September was a dry run for Seattle, minus the EU. The accommodation reached there provides an indicator of the likely parameters of the Millennium Round negotiations. The Leaders' Declaration called for a new round that would:

- "include comprehensive market access negotiations covering industrial tariffs in addition to the already mandated negotiations on services and agriculture"
- "lead to timely and effective improvements in market access to the benefit of all participating economies, particularly developing economies, and"
- "consistent with this objective, provide scope to review and strengthen rules and disciplines,"
- "have a balanced and sufficiently broad-based agenda and be concluded within three years as a single package which does not preclude the possibility of early results on a provisional basis"
- "have, as one of the important objectives of the negotiations on agriculture, the abolition of export subsidies."

This language of the declaration was carefully crafted to embrace the positions of all the participants, particularly the Americans and the Japanese. The Japanese desire for comprehensive, single undertaking negotiation was accepted without precluding the possibility of an early harvest of provisional sectoral agreements as was sought by the United States. Such sectoral agreements could include those covered by the Accelerated Tariff Liberalization initiative, which the United States is pushing and which had its origin in APEC's EVSL initiative. The sectors covered are: chemicals; energy equipment; environmental goods; fish and fishery products; gems and jewelry; medical equipment and scientific instruments; toys; and forest products. Japan has dug in its heels in the fish and forest products sectors.

A three-year time frame was endorsed in the Declaration reflecting the American objective of keeping the negotiations "manageable." It probably represents wishful thinking given the number and complexity of the issues likely to be on the table. But it is necessary to set an ambitious timetable to make sure that the negotiations don't go on forever like the Uruguay Round. This time however, with the WTO and its permanent committee structure in existence, it will be possible to continue negotiations on some issues, on which it is impossible to reach agreement, in a sort of "rolling negotiation."

The need to abolish agricultural export subsidies and prohibitions and restrictions was emphasized. This is an objective that is strongly supported by

APEC agricultural exporting countries like the United States, Canada, Australia and New Zealand and by some of the ASEAN agricultural exporting countries. It was much less enthusiastically embraced by Japan, a country that is known for its protectionist agricultural policies. It also won't be welcomed in Europe whose Common Agricultural Policy is its chief target.

The question of modalities for the market access negotiations was left open. They could be zero/zero initiatives, proportional, offer-request, harmonization, or peak tariff cuts. Nothing was said about the desirability of lowering bound tariff rates to the level of applied tariffs.

No mention was made of the American objective of doing something on core labour standards and the environment. The developing countries of Asia, and even Japan, don't see any need to do anything in these controversial areas. There is a concern that any such initiatives could easily turn into some form of disguised protectionism to their disadvantage.

In its informal paper on the Millennium Round, the EU also accepted the need for a comprehensive three-year round covering the built-in agenda of agriculture and services as well as industrial tariffs. The EU argued in favour of a single undertaking, but allowed the possibility of an early harvest as long as the final package did not become unbalanced.

Agriculture is an area where the EU parts company from the APEC consensus. The EU's negotiating position for agriculture, which was approved in September by agricultural ministers, calls for a defence of production subsidies. The rationale is that domestic producers with higher production costs resulting from superior standards of animal welfare or environmental protection need to be protected from low-cost competition. The EU also seeks rules on the use of export credit guarantees.

Still smarting from the loss of the recent WTO panel decision on hormone-treated beef and facing consumer concerns about the health risks of genetically modified foods, the EU will be trying to make its approach to food regulation WTO-consistent. This will entail seeking more recognition of the legitimacy of the precautionary principle in regulating foods and/or some weakening of the science test that must be met to ban foods considered hazardous to health. The US and Canada, which were on the winning side of the WTO case, can be expected to resist.

The US and EU will be seeking more market access in the service sector. But the EU is calling for "cultural diversity" to be taken into account in liberalizing the trade in audio-visual services.

The US initiative to develop an Agreement on Transparency in Government Procurement seems to have been proceeding well. It will likely be an early harvest of the Millennium Round at Seattle.

The US, which proposed the moratorium on tariffs on e-commerce, has been championing a permanent elimination of tariffs and barriers. Other countries are likely to go along with the proposal as long as e-commerce is defined narrowly enough, but the devil will be in the details.

Investment is a very sensitive issue politically in the United States and Europe. While there is a recognition of the benefits to be derived from multilateral rules for investment, there is also a reluctance to push the issue too hard lest it stir up the same sort of opposition that scuttled the MAI negotiations and jeopardize other objectives of the Millennium Round. Japan is pushing more actively for an investment agreement. It has proposed a bottom-up approach to the agreement such as was employed in the Uruguay Round service sector negotiations. Under this approach, countries have to make specific commitments with respect to particular sectors. Japan has also proposed that national treatment only be extended on a post-establishment basis and that the agreement not allow for investor-state disputes. The EU had a similar proposal, but is soft pedaling it, out of fear of a repeat of the MAI.

The EU is seeking to establish a common multilateral framework of rules and principles for competition policy. This is a new and complex area that is not a high priority in the United States and might meet resistance from that quarter if it seems likely to delay the conclusion of the round.

Japan is very keen on negotiating additional disciplines on anti-dumping. The recent application of US anti-dumping actions to the Japanese steel industry has reinforced its desire.

The EU is even more aggressive than the US in pushing for action on trade and the environment. But while the EU favours a strong statement on protecting labour rights and is calling for a new "forum" to monitor labour standards, it is against the use of trade measures to encourage the observance of core labour standards. Instead, it prefers a "more cooperative and consensus-oriented approach" that includes the use positive measures.

There is also a lot of housekeeping that needs to be done to make sure that all the Uruguay Round agreements are working as they should and that all of the commitments are being honoured.

Table 3
Summary of Positions of Quad Countries on Key Issues in Negotiating Agenda

	United States	European Union	Japan	Canada
Three-year time frame	yes	yes	yes	?
Single Undertaking	if can be kept "managable"	yes	yes	?
Early Sectoral Results	Accelerated Tariff Liberalization for 8 sectors	as long as package doesn't become unbalanced	concerned about forestry and fishing	?
Agricultural Subsidies	cut	defends	not so enthusiastic about cutting	Cut, but wants to preserve orderly marketing arrangements and farm support programs
Food Standards	Should be based on science, balance of risk	Precautionary principle	?	Should be based on science, balance of risk
Fishery and forestry	early harvest liberalization	?	not appropriate to isolate	early harvest liberalization
Services	Improved access	Improved access, but take account of "cultural diversity" for audio-visual services	?	Concerned about culture
Transparency in Government Procurement	Strongly support as early harvest	support	support	?

Table 3 (continued)
Summary of Positions of Quad Countries on Key Issues in Negotiating Agenda

	United States	European Union	Japan	Canada
E-Commerce	No tariffs or barriers	goes along	goes along	goes along
Trade Remedies	opposed to more disciplines	status quo	more disciplines	?
Investment	if doesn't get in the way of other issues	not too ambitious given previous failure at OECD	bottom-up approach to admission, post-establishment national treatment with no investor state	?
Competition Policy	concerned could stall negotiations	yes	?	?
Environment	yes	yes	no	?
Labour standards	yes	yes, but no trade sanctions, forum	no	?

CANADA'S ROLE

There are so many question marks in Table 3 regarding Canada's position on the key Millennium Round negotiating issues because at the time this book was being written Canada had not yet released an overall position paper. It's not that no effort was made to study the issues. A discussion paper entitled *Opening Doors to the World* released in March by the Minister of International Trade launched an ambitious round of public consultations spearheaded by the House of Commons Standing Committee on Foreign Affairs and International Trade. The Committee issued its report *Canada at the WTO: Towards a Millennium Agenda* in June which provided the Government with detailed, if somewhat vague, recommendations. The Canadian government has also provided nine communications on specific issues to the WTO General Council, which provide some information on Canada's position on a few of the issues.

It's unfortunate that Canada could not take the process that final step to produce an official position paper well before Seattle as the United States and the EU did. In the past Canada's influence in trade negotiations, which in the jargon of boxing enabled us to fight above our weight, stemmed from an uncanny ability to come up with creative positions on controversial issues early in the negotiations before the positions of the other players had crystalized. This time Canada will have to play more of a role as a mediator or an honest broker to exercise the same kind of influence.

Canada will also need to get better prepared to deal with sectoral and industrial issues. During the FTA, Uruguay Round and NAFTA negotiations, an International Trade Advisory Committee (ITAC) and Sectoral Advisory Groups on International Trade (SAGITs) provided a unique business and labour perspective on negotiating priorities and strategies, that helped the Government to negotiate more effectively. The ITAC has been replaced by the Team Canada Inc. Advisory Board whose mandate is export promotion, not trade negotiations, and the SAGITs are dormant with a few exceptions such as agriculture and culture. These groups need to be resurrected to provide the Government with the kind of focussed business and labour input on overall and sectoral trade issues that it will require to successfully negotiate for Canada in the Millennium Round.

Finally, Canada will have to decide who is really going to be responsible for trade policy if it is going to play a leading role in the upcoming negotiations. Provincial governments seem to be unwilling to let the federal government speak for Canada. Quebec wants a seat at the negotiating table and Alberta wants a larger role in the negotiations. The provincial governments have already prevented Canadian businesses from getting access to procurement opportunities in sub-federal governments under the GPA. This is totally unacceptable. The provinces should limit their participation in trade negotiations to making sure that their legitimate concerns in their own areas of jurisdiction such as health and social policy are respected. They should not try to dictate the federal negotiating position.

DEVELOPING COUNTRIES

The developing countries, which are still having difficulties coming to grips with the disciplines of the Uruguay Round agreements and commitments, are not as enthusiastic about a new round as the Quad and other industrialized countries. India opposes a new round outright and Malaysia would like to see the start of the round postponed until after 2000. But since there is likely to be a round whether they like it or not, developing countries have to be ready. Consequently, seventeen developing countries came together as the misnomered G15 to prepare a joint negotiating agenda at a meeting in Bangalore, India in August. They will be seeking to improve market access for their products in developed countries' markets. In particular, they will be targeting developed country tariffs on many manufactured goods produced in developing countries which are still relatively high. They will also benefit from any improved access to the huge European agricultural market that the United States is able to extract. Developing countries will also be defending their hard-won benefits from previous rounds. The big Uruguay-Round prize for developing countries, which might come under attack around the edges if China accedes to the WTO, is the phased elimination of the Multi-Fibre Arrangement.

The developing countries will also face increased demands from the developed world. This will include pressure for additional reductions in the very high tariff rates levied by developing countries and tougher enforcement of the TRIPs Agreement. There will also be pressure on the developing countries to go along with whatever is negotiated with respect to environment and labour standards. This is something the G15 vowed to resist in Bangalore.

The developing countries that are best placed to benefit from the Millennium Round are the least developed countries, of which thirty are WTO Members. Michael Moore, the new WTO Director General, has declared himself their champion and is pushing for guaranteed duty-free access for all their exports. This picks up a proposal initially put forward by the EU. It has now made its way into the Draft Ministerial Declaration, at least with square brackets indicating it is on the table and requires a political decision at the Ministerial. As the least developed countries count for less that ¾ per cent of world trade, according them duty-free access should not threaten industry in the developed countries. But the United States reportedly wants to maintain its system granting duty-free access based on their human rights record. Moore also wants to make more technical assistance available so that these countries can participate more fully in the WTO and comply with their WTO obligations. He is likely to get a sympathetic hearing from the Quad countries on his proposals as the US and the EU have already recognized the need in their pre-Seattle discussion papers.

OUR MILLENNIUM ROUND WISH LIST

In our view, a successful Millennium Round would include:

- *Tariffs* Reductions averaging of at least a third and elimination of nuisance tariffs below 2 or 3 per cent.
- *Non-Tariff Barriers* Significant progress in decreasing NTBs, including most notably the negotiation of an Agreement on Trade Facilitation.
- *Agriculture* The elimination of export subsidies. Drastic cuts in production subsidies. Large decreases in high tariff rates established through tariffication. Improved minimum market-access commitments. Acceptance of precautionary principle for foods such as hormone-treated beef and genetically modified crops.
- *Services* Expansion of market access commitments to include a much broader range of services. Getting all WTO Members to sign on to the agreements on Financial Services and Basic Telecommunications.
- *Government Procurement* A new Agreement on Transparency in Government Procurement reached at Seattle. Expansion of the coverage of the Government Procurement Agreement to include more signatories and more government sector entities for existing signatories. Ideally, a multilateral agreement to replace the existing plurilateral one. Canadian commitments for provincial and local government procurement.
- *E-commerce* An agreement on e-commerce including a permanent moratorium on tariffs on the international transmission of digitalized information.
- *Subsidies and Countervailing Measures* Stronger disciplines on subsidies and countervailing measures. Extending coverage to services.
- *Investment* A bottom-up agreement based on commitments by individual countries providing post-establishment national treatment and offering investor protection, but providing no mechanism for investor-state dispute settlement.
- *Intellectual Property* Full compliance with intellectual property obligations under TRIPs.
- *Culture* Clarification of whether cultural products are covered by GATT or GATS. Rules to permit domestic subsidies to a narrowly defined cultural sector.
- *Environment* Amendment to Article XX of the GATT to permit trade measures authorized under Multilateral Environmental Agreements.
- *Labour Standards* The creation of some joint WTO-ILO mechanism to monitor and report on the implementation of core labour standards.
- *Dispute Settlement Mechanism* Improved transparency and an opening up of access to panel proceedings to non-participating governments and the public. Elimination of the delay in the release of panel decisions.

- *Accession* Getting China into the WTO in time to participate fully in the Millennium Round.
- *Developing Countries* Removal of tariffs on imports from least developed countries. The provision of technical assistance to assist in the implementation of WTO agreements. Financial assistance to least developed countries to participate in the WTO.

WORLD TRADE IN THE 21ST CENTURY

The WTO Millennium Round is critical for the future of the world trading system. Since World War II, great progress has been made under the GATT/WTO in bringing down tariffs, and eradicating trade barriers. The global economy that has sprung up is a powerful engine of economic growth. It has created prosperity in the advanced industrialized countries of the world and fostered economic development in the developing world, thus reducing poverty. Continued material progress depends on the preservation and expansion of the WTO-managed multilateral trading system. And global free trade is only a couple of more successful WTO rounds away.

The WTO has come under unprecedented attack from the forces that would turn back the clock of globalization and retreat into the protectionist shells of their national economies. And it's not only the protest groups. Faced with the Asian crisis and growing trade deficits in some countries, some governments have taken protectionist steps. These misguided forces of protectionism must be resisted.

The new round provides an opportunity to enter the new millennium with a renewed international commitment to a truly global, rules-based international trading system that will provide a sound framework the functioning of markets. The achievement of this vision, which inspired all those that have participated in the GATT/WTO, offers the best prospect of a prosperous and peaceful global economy in the 21st century.

Selected Bibliography

Browne, Dennis (ed.) (1998) *The Culture/Trade Quandary: Canada's Policy Options* (Ottawa: Centre for Trade Policy and Law).

Department of Finance (1988) *The Canada-U.S. Free Trade Agreement: An Economic Assessment* (Ottawa).

Department of Finance (1994) *The Uruguay Round of the General Agreement on Tariffs and Trade: An Assessment of the Economic Impact on Canada* (Ottawa).

Department of Foreign Affairs and International Trade (1999) *Consultation Paper on WTO/FTAA Investment* (Ottawa).

Department of Foreign Affairs and International Trade (1999) *Opening Doors to the World: Canada's International Market Access Priorities 1999* (Ottawa).

Hart, Michael (1998) *Fifty Years of Canadian Tradecraft: Canada at the GATT 1947-1997* (Ottawa: Centre for Trade Policy and Law).

House of Commons, Standing Committee on Foreign Affairs and International Trade (1999) *Canada and the World Trade Organization: Advancing a Millennium Agenda in the Public Interest: Report*, June.

Howse, Robert (1998) "Settling Trade Disputes: When the WTO Forum is Better Than The NAFTA," *C.D. Howe Institute Commentary 111* (Toronto).

Inside US Trade (1999) "Barshefsky Reveals US Push to Broaden WTO Service Talks," June 4.

Inside US Trade (1999b) "Draft WTO Declaration Omits Key Issues for Many Members," October 15.

Johnson, Jon R. (1998) *International Trade Law* (Concord, Ontario: Irwin Law).

Josling, Timothy (1998) *Agricultural Trade Policy: Completing the Reform* (Washington, D.C.: Institute for International Economics).

Milazzo, Mateo (1998) "Subsidies in World Fisheries: A Re-examination", *World Bank Technical Paper No. 406*, Fisheries Series (Washington).

Organisation for Economic Cooperation and Development (1997) *Indicators of Tariff and Non-Tariff Trade Barriers: Update 1997* (Paris).

Sachs, Jeffrey and Andrew Warner (1995) "Economic Reform and the Process of Global Integration," *Brookings Papers on Economic Activity*, 0(1), pp.1-95.

Sachs, Jeffrey (1999) "Helping the World's Poorest," *The Economist*, August 14, pp.17-20.

Schott, Jeffrey J. (ed.) (1998) *Launching New Global Trade Talks: An Action Agenda* (Washington, D.C.: Institute for International Economics).

Schwanen, Daniel (1997) "A Matter of Choice: Toward a More Creative Canadian Policy on Culture," *C.D. Howe Institute Commentary 91* (Toronto).

The Cultural Industries Sectoral Advisory Group on International Trade *(1999) Canadian Culture in a Global World* (Ottawa).

The Economist (1999) "Business and the Internet," June 26.

The Economist (1999) "Why greens should love trade," October 9.

The Economist (1998) "World Trade," October 3.

United States Trade Representative (1998) *1998 Annual Report* (Washington D.C.).

World Trade Organization (1994) *The Results of the Uruguay Round of Multilateral Trade Negotiations: the Legal Texts* (Geneva).

World Trade Organization (1998) *Annual Report* (Geneva).

World Trade Organization (1998) *Electronic Commerce and the Role of the WTO* (Geneva).

Index